THE
ASSESSMENT
PLAYBOOK FOR
DISTANCE
& BLENDED
LEARNING

THE ASSESSMENT PLAYBOOK FOR DISTANCE & BLENDED LEARNING

MEASURING STUDENT LEARNING IN ANY SETTING

DOUGLAS FISHER · NANCY FREY · VINCE BUSTAMANTE · JOHN HATTIE

FOR INFORMATION:

Corwin

A SAGE Company

2455 Teller Road

Thousand Oaks, California 91320

(800) 233-9936

www.corwin.com

SAGE Publications Ltd.

1 Oliver's Yard

55 City Road

London EC1Y 1SP

United Kingdom

SAGE Publications India Pvt. Ltd.

B 1/I 1 Mohan Cooperative Industrial Area

Mathura Road, New Delhi 110 044

India

SAGE Publications Asia-Pacific Pte. Ltd.

18 Cross Street #10-10/11/12

China Square Central

Singapore 048423

Director and Publisher,
Corwin Classroom: Lisa Luedeke

Editorial Development Manager: Julie Nemer

Associate Content
Development Editor: Sharon Wu

Production Editor: Melanie Birdsall

Copy Editor: Diane DiMura

Typesetter: C&M Digitals (P) Ltd.

Proofreader: Susan Schon

Indexer: Sheila Hill

Cover and Interior Designer: Gail Buschman

Marketing Manager: Deena Meyer

Printed in the United States of America

ISBN 978-1-0718-4536-3

Library of Congress Control Number: 2020921136

This book is printed on acid-free paper.

20 21 22 23 24 10 9 8 7 6 5 4 3 2 1

Contents

Visit the companion website at
resources.corwin.com/AssessmentPlaybook
for downloadable resources and videos.

List of Videos

Note From the Publisher: The authors have provided video and web content throughout the book that is available to you through QR (quick response) codes. To read a QR code, you must have a smartphone or tablet with a camera. We recommend that you download a QR code reader app that is made specifically for your phone or tablet brand.

Videos may also be accessed at **resources.corwin.com/AssessmentPlaybook**

Dear Colleagues,

Schooling has changed considerably over a very short period of time. In a matter of months, teachers and students have engaged in physical distancing, social isolation, and enhanced safety protocols. Yet schools remained a tried and true institution. Teachers and students were forced into new and different learning environments and while the rest of the world came to a screeching halt, schools persevered through unimaginable times. This highly commendable "pivot" should not go uncelebrated. Through the collective efforts of all those involved in education, students received the best possible learning experience in an emergency situation. In other words, we did what we could with what we had.

When the new school year started, the world still found itself in a mode of relative panic. Schools did not. Staff and students across the world collectively drew a line in the sand and broke away from the "pandemic teaching of spring 2020" and engaged in a new school year that presented unique challenges. "To be clear, the pandemic teaching of [spring] 2020 was really not distance learning. It was also not homeschooling, which is a choice parents make for very specific reasons (e.g, religious, safety, not happy with their public school). It was crisis teaching" (Fisher, Frey, & Hattie, 2020, p. 1).

At the beginning of the new school year, teachers found themselves teaching in new environments and new ways. Some teachers are exclusively teaching online classes from home, some are engaging in socially distanced face-to-face learning, and others are engaging in a hybridization of both of those models. Regardless of which teaching environment we may find ourselves teaching in, one fundamental truth remains: We must consider what works best for student learning.

In an ever-changing educational landscape, we are now tasked with leading our students through a variety of learning experiences that have some (if not all) aspects of distance learning embedded within them. The fidelity we put toward the implementation of distance learning will pay dividends in the future. We are engaging in important work, and now is the time to be more purposeful and intentional with distance learning. Not only is this important now, but as our world continues to navigate through crises, pandemics, and other emergency situations, teachers will consistently be tasked with adapting their teaching.

Every day in class sessions teachers are making judgments and evaluating what are the next best teaching decisions. They observe, listen, talk to, and engage with students to diagnose and discover their progress, their understandings and misunderstandings. They assign tasks and tests and from this understand what they taught well and not so well, who gained from the teaching and who did not, and appreciate how much learning or not enough learning has taken place. These are all the core of "assessment," and in teaching during COVID, this task becomes even more critical. Many of the usual cues and opportunities are not so available when students are not in front of us and we can walk the room, so we need to discover alternative ways to keep this form of evidence coming to teachers from their students.

As we look to shift our practice to a distance learning model, it is paramount that we do not forget about this important role of assessment. Assessments, when done properly, can serve to inform both the student and the teacher about the impact a specific strategy has on student learning and achievement. The challenge we face now is in designing assessments that appropriately measure and target student learning both in face-to-face and distance learning environments.

That brings us to the purpose of this book. The reality is that assessments used in face-to-face environments are not always the most impactful or practical in distance learning. This book serves to provide examples, strategies, and assessments that can be leveraged with rigor and fidelity regardless of learning environment. We seek to leverage the expertise and experiences of those teachers who are currently engaging in distance learning and experiencing success.

Our wish is that you see assessments as handmaidens to the all-important evaluative thinking that teachers engage in. Assessments can be part of adjusting how we see the evidence of each student's progress to higher achievement, as part of the evidence to critique or complement our observations and judgments while in the act of teaching, and as part of understanding the impact we are having on students. Assessments fulfill a critical role in these evaluations, and this places a premium on the quality of the interpretations we make from assessments. Assessments are not about the numbers, not about the grades and comments, but are about informing us and students about their progress and should lead to the very best next teaching actions. If we as teachers learn nothing or too little from students' assessments about our impact (about what for whom, and how much), then these same assessments are probably not using student time and energies most effectively. And if students do not learn from assessments their next best learning moves, then we have a major job to teach them to become better interpreters of their test information.

Our hope is that you take the experiences of teachers highlighted in this book and apply the strategies with the understanding that we are building an educational future that is not considered "distance learning for now." When designed properly, assessments implemented through the lens of distance learning can yield significant impact on student learning and in many cases will transcend the learning environment in which they are applied.

Our intention is to provide teachers with assessments that can be applied in current and future contexts. While designing high-quality assessments in a distance learning environment may appear daunting, we hope that by leveraging the strategies presented in this book that teachers everywhere will engage in high impact strategies. We also hope that you will discover how powerful some of these methods are while teaching from a distance and then consider how to adapt them when the students finally return to the in-class instruction.

Doug, Nancy, Vince, and John

iStock/Maria Symchych-Navrotska

Assessments are not about the numbers, but about informing us and our students about their progress.

Introduction

Assessment is the link between teaching and learning. As such, assessment should be part of every lesson that teachers plan, distance or otherwise. In particular, assessment data should be analyzed to gauge what is known already, what has been fully learned, what is only partially understood, and where errors and misconceptions stubbornly remain, and to enjoy the discovery of student mastery. Robust assessment systems allow teachers to make informed decisions about their impact and to adjust the learning experiences of students based on the evidence they collect. In essence, assessments provide teachers an opportunity to be an evaluator of their impact and can guide the future instruction that students experience. Consider the following two classes in middle school (and we recognize that you don't all teach middle school):

These two classes are at the same school, but they might as well be on different planets. On the surface they seem comparable; both are led by experienced and caring teachers. Their interactions with students during synchronous meetings are warm and inviting. They each utilize good curriculum materials and both present organized and engaging lessons. They both check for understanding, invite chat responses, and use hand signals. Yet the students perform academically in significantly different ways, despite the fact that the students in both classes are academically and socially similar. In the lower performing class, the teacher focuses on covering content. Students receive grades for projects and homework. In addition, quizzes are scored automatically by the learning management system and tests are adopted from a commercially available system. Evaluations of student learning are administered only one time, and students do not have the opportunity to correct them, analyze errors, or improve on their initial attempts. It's "one and done" in this class.

But in the higher-performing classroom, the teacher views assessment as the engine of learning. Assessments are used for learning and as learning tools. This teacher provides students opportunities to complete the quizzes and tests, along with the projects, but students are tasked with analyzing their own performance, their success, and their errors and are directed to review materials in order to correct them and undertake the next best set of learning challenges. These self-assessments are transformed into goals established in partnership with the teacher. To accomplish their goals, students engage in additional study, often asynchronously, to deepen their understanding. They know that the quizzes and practice tests are not used in their grades, but rather as opportunities to determine additional learning needed. Instead, their grades are based on summaries of their learning that are recorded and shared with the teacher, as well as on the projects they complete.

Perhaps most importantly, the teacher in the high-performing class uses a competency-based system to evaluate students' learning. When teachers make success criteria transparent to students as they start a series of lessons, these help establish the criteria of success, the desired levels of mastery. Students who do not

Vince Bustamante introduces *The Assessment Playbook for Distance and Blended Learning.*

resources.corwin.com/ AssessmentPlaybook

To read a QR code, you must have a smartphone or tablet with a camera. We recommend that you download a QR code reader app that is made specifically for your phone or tablet brand.

earn a passing grade of (say) 70 percent receive an Incomplete rather than a failing grade. The students in this class have learned that it is essential to master each part of the curriculum, not simply hope that the law of averages will result in a passing grade for the course. In some ways, this is more work for the teacher, who must prepare multiple forms of an assessment. In addition, students with Incompletes must successfully complete review materials tailored to the concepts underlying the items they missed before they can take a new version of the assessment. But the results are astounding. The learning of students in the second class, measured by a summative evaluation developed by the school system and administered to all students in the course, is much better than those in the first one. They actually learned from their experiences with assessments.

Teachers should determine their impact on students' learning, and a variety of assessment tools can help them do so. In this book, we provide a wide range of assessment tools that you can use to determine students' learning (and your impact) and then use that information in your decision-making, whether that be for future instruction or for determining impact and grades. The examples come from distance and blended learning but have implications for all classrooms. A positive is that the pandemic has allowed teachers to rethink assessment and develop new tools that inform their work.

In the first section of this book, Assessment Cookies, we focus on some enduring aspects of assessment from a distance. This section includes the following:

1. Assessment is difficult because it is important.

2. Assessments come in all shapes and sizes.

3. Know the learner and their learning journey.

4. Assess that which has been taught and teach based on the standards.

5. Students deserve to know what they should be learning.

6. Knowing your destination helps.

7. Everything is searchable, so plan accordingly.

8. Parents want to help and sometimes it's problematic.

Remember, if the assessment does not help the teacher learn about their impact, then it needs to change.

The second section of this book, The Playlists, focuses on your assessment tools that we have organized into a playlist of sorts. This section includes

1. Universal response

2. Teach-back opportunities

3. Composing

4. Self-assessment and peer assessment

> THE CHALLENGE WE FACE NOW IS IN DESIGNING ASSESSMENTS THAT APPROPRIATELY MEASURE AND TARGET STUDENT LEARNING BOTH IN FACE-TO-FACE AND DISTANCE LEARNING ENVIRONMENTS.

The final section of this book focuses on upgrading your assessments and thinking like an evaluator. In this final section, we'll focus on the use of more formal tools that can be used to document learning for reporting purposes. We will consider characteristics of longer essays, tests, and performance tasks that are commonly used to determine proficiency, competency, or mastery of learning. We include performance assessments, ipsative assessments (what a cool word, right? Are you excited to learn more?), confirmative assessments, and thinking like an evaluator.

istock/Fabio Principe

Students in high-performing classrooms are tasked with analyzing their own performance, their successes, and their errors.

1 ASSESSMENT COOKIES

This first section focuses on some enduring lessons related to assessment. We think of these as "assessment cookies," or bits of advice that stick with you. When you visit a website, a small piece of data is stored for future use. These cookies are designed to be a reliable way for the system to remember something. Cookies consist of information and help the computer operate. And just like the dessert, not all cookies are good. But when they are, they're very helpful. In this section, we suggest some helpful assessment cookies, or bits of information, that can help you make decisions about assessments.

In this section:

- ☐ ASSESSMENT IS DIFFICULT BECAUSE IT IS IMPORTANT
- ☐ ASSESSMENTS COME IN ALL SHAPES AND SIZES
- ☐ KNOW THE LEARNER AND THEIR LEARNING JOURNEY
- ☐ ASSESS THAT WHICH HAS BEEN TAUGHT AND TEACH BASED ON THE STANDARDS
- ☐ STUDENTS DESERVE TO KNOW WHAT THEY SHOULD BE LEARNING
- ☐ KNOWING YOUR DESTINATION HELPS
- ☐ EVERYTHING IS SEARCHABLE, SO PLAN ACCORDINGLY
- ☐ PARENTS WANT TO HELP AND SOMETIMES IT'S PROBLEMATIC

ASSESSMENT COOKIE 1: ASSESSMENT IS DIFFICULT BECAUSE IT IS IMPORTANT

Designing high-quality assessments is not an easy task. Creating assessments can be messy. And distance learning environments didn't help make assessment easier. Teachers often report that assessing students online takes significantly more effort than assessing students in person. A number of questions come into play when we attempt to assess a student's current level of understanding, including the following:

➡ Will this assessment evaluate skills or content knowledge (or both)?

➡ Will this assessment evaluate the process or product?

➡ What form will this assessment be (project, quiz, exit ticket, etc.)?

➡ Will this assessment be open book or closed book?

➡ What biases could exist in the assessment?

➡ Is the assessment based on what has been taught or are students using their knowledge from other aspects of their life?

➡ Can I use the information from the assessment to support future learning for students?

➡ Can I use the information from the assessment to determine my impact?

  Available for download at **resources.corwin.com/AssessmentPlaybook**

These considerations, among others, are reasons why designing assessments is time and energy consuming. Nonetheless, assessments remain important. In fact, they are one of the major job responsibilities that teachers have. Our role is not to simply provide information. One of our requirements is to determine whether or not students have learned and then report that information to others, such as on report cards and transcripts (yes, there are many other purposes of assessment). And these permanent records can impact students' lives, such as services they receive, how their parents think about their children's success, and even which colleges offer admissions. There are a significant number of ways that report cards and grades influence the future of our students. It's an important responsibility we have and one that we should take seriously. The importance of assessment has not been reduced in distance and blended learning; if anything, it is heightened. One of the considerations for the assessments we design and use focuses on rigor. We have to ask ourselves if we are assessing students based on the content they are expected to learn.

Rigor:
Difficulty Versus Complexity

To our thinking, rigor is comprised of two factors. The first is difficulty, which includes the amount of time, work, or effort that is required to complete a task. The second is complexity of the thinking that is required. This may include background knowledge, relating pieces of information, or problem-solving through multiple steps. Rigor requires both complexity and difficulty, and not difficulty alone. Consider the following assessment item:

Which of these means about the same as the word *gauge*?

a. balance

b. measure

c. select

d. warn

Not much complexity there, but some students will find it difficult based on their age, familiarity with the English language, and previous learning. Should students know the word? Sure. But there are so many other ways to determine understanding of key terminology. As we discuss various tools, we'll return to this idea of balancing difficulty with complexity. We hope that teachers do not simply develop assessments that are hard and time consuming, but rather tools that allow students to engage in thinking and problem-solving. Figure 1 highlights attributes of rigorous and relevant curriculum (standards). As you read through these, reflect on how assessments can be created to support these understandings.

1 KEY UNDERSTANDINGS OF A RIGOROUS AND RELEVANT CURRICULUM

Rigorous and relevant learning experiences

- Are directly applicable to students' lives

- Ask students to use skills including active learning, problem solving, and reasoning to demonstrate their understanding of the learning outcomes

- Are based on rigorous and relevant curriculum that often requires students to make connections between disciplines

- Focus on the application of concepts and skills in a real-world context

- Incorporate teaching materials and assessment strategies aligned with the curriculum's rigor and relevance

- Include teachers who support and encourage students to meet the high standards set for them

Source: ©Alberta Education. *High School Completion; Moving Forward with High School Redesign; High School Redesign Foundational Principals; Rigorous and Relevant Curriculum.* Edmonton, AB. 2011. https://www.alberta.ca/high-school-completion.aspx

Screenshots

➡ Assessments are an important part of the teaching and learning process.

➡ Assessments should reflect what students have learned.

➡ Rigor is an important consideration in learning and assessment.

ASSESSMENT COOKIE 2: ASSESSMENTS COME IN ALL SHAPES AND SIZES

Assessments come in different sizes. What we mean by assessment *size* is the consideration of time spent completing the assessment (both synchronously and asynchronously), as well as how much student effort is required to complete this assessment. The assessment size requires consideration about what the student and teacher will *do* with the assessment both during and after the time frame they have engaged with it. If teachers and students are unsure of the purpose of the assessment, then we argue the assessment is not appropriate in time and place.

For example, asking a question and inviting students to respond via chat is a relatively small assessment. Having students complete a task in which they summarize what they have learned over the course of a week via a Flipgrid video is a larger assessment. Assigning a project that includes multiple components and a written response is even larger. This size consideration is important as time will need to be allocated accordingly. Figure 2 contains several questions for consideration as you plan assessments.

> IF TEACHERS AND STUDENTS ARE UNSURE OF THE PURPOSE OF THE ASSESSMENT, THEN WE ARGUE THE ASSESSMENT IS NOT APPROPRIATE IN TIME AND PLACE.

2 REFLECTION QUESTIONS IN ASSESSMENT MAPPING

☐ What size assessment will I be using?

☐ Does this assessment inform me about students' performance?

☐ Does this assessment inform students about their performance?

☐ Does this assessment focus on a product?

☐ Does this assessment focus on processes?

☐ Do students have voice and choice in the production of this assessment?

☐ How will I inform my students (or how will my students inform each other) of their evaluation?

☐ How am I measuring progress/achievement on this assessment?

 Available for download at **resources.corwin.com/AssessmentPlaybook**

The shape and size consideration also influences what can be done with the assessment. The practice of engaging in high-quality assessments should not stop once the teacher has assigned something to students. If students complete an assessment for a grade, chances are they will not engage in any self-reevaluation once they receive their assessment back. Figure 3 contains three definitions that are used at Edmonton Catholic Schools to define types of assessment (Assessment *for, as,* and *of* learning). These definitions, first advanced as part of the Assessment Reform Group in the United Kingdom, can serve as consideration when creating assessments. Considering the simple question, *What will I do with the assessment information?* can serve as a guidepost for both students and teachers.

3 USES OF ASSESSMENT

- **Assessment *for* learning:** The process involving ongoing, frequent, and purposeful exchange of information between students and teachers about student progress toward clearly specific learning goals, for the purpose of improving learning and informing instruction; formative assessment includes opportunities for students to practice and demonstrate their understanding and skills prior to summative assessment.

- **Assessment *as* learning:** Engaging students in a process of setting criteria, using self-assessment against establish criteria, and goal setting, through the design and modelling of metacognitive strategies.

- **Assessment *of* learning:** Assessment experience is designed to collect information about learning and make judgments about student performance and achievement at the end of a period instruction; maybe in the form of a grade, descriptors on a rubric or level of achievement.

Source: Edmonton Catholic Schools. AP 360 document.

IF STUDENTS COMPLETE AN ASSESSMENT FOR A GRADE, CHANCES ARE THEY WILL NOT ENGAGE IN ANY SELF-REEVALUATION ONCE THEY RECEIVE THEIR ASSESSMENT BACK.

Despite the common language to the contrary, there is no "formative assessment" and there is no "summative assessment." This false dichotomy has been problematic. Essentially, any assessment could be used formatively or summatively. Some are better for one or the other, but a teacher could use a letter recognition test summatively and state test scores formatively. This dichotomy has prevented educators from thinking about all of the information they have and using that information as evaluators, specifically evaluators of their impact on students' learning. In the final section of this book, we'll focus on evaluative thinking and the use of assessments for that purpose. Thus, we cannot make a simple list of tools that are used *for, as,* and *of* learning. Our point is that the purpose should be clear before choosing the size and type of assessment.

Choosing an assessment *size* before an assessment *type* is important. Knowing how much time you want students to spend on the assessment and what you, and your students, will do with the assessment impacts the types of assessments you can use. Careful consideration of the size of assessment provides you the opportunity to monitor and adjust based on learners' progress. In other words, assessment size and the use of the data that follows, allows for appropriate scaffolds for success. In distance learning, students must be provided with as many opportunities to demonstrate their learning in a rigorous and relevant environment as possible. After all, learning is our goal, not compliance in completing a task.

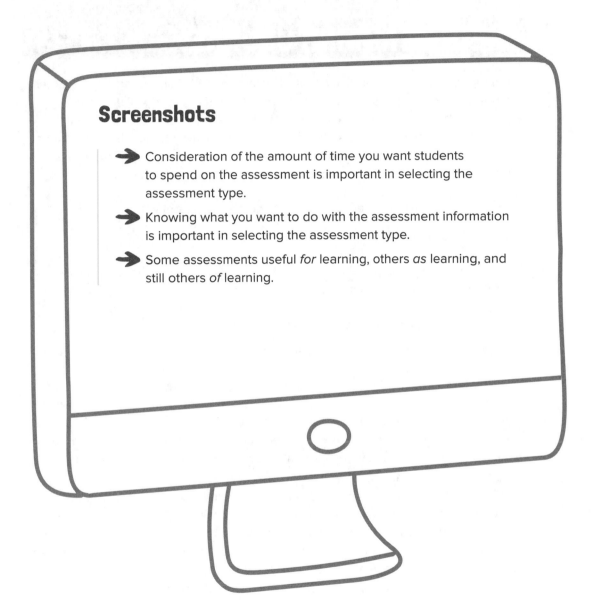

Screenshots

→ Consideration of the amount of time you want students to spend on the assessment is important in selecting the assessment type.

→ Knowing what you want to do with the assessment information is important in selecting the assessment type.

→ Some assessments useful *for* learning, others *as* learning, and still others *of* learning.

ASSESSMENT COOKIE 3: KNOW THE LEARNER AND THEIR LEARNING JOURNEY

To paraphrase the late Rita Pierson and her famous TED Talk, young people do not learn from older people they do not like. It's unlikely that any significant learning will occur in the absence of a significant relationship. In other words, it's important to know your learners, and for them to know you. Knowing them as individuals, knowing their names, and knowing things about them are all important. In distance learning, it's also important to know where the student is learning. You might consider the following:

➡ Does the student have a place to focus on their learning?

➡ Who else is in their environment with them?

In addition, it may be important to consider social and emotional impacts on learning (and thus assessment performance) such as these:

➡ Are they themselves anxious, uncertain, or ill?

➡ Do they feel safe emotionally and physically?

The answers to each of these questions can impact the ways in which assessment information is used. We are not suggesting that we lower learning expectations for some students but rather that we consider their current realities and allocate unequal resources for unequal needs. Knowing your students allows you to contextualize the results of assessments and to take action based on the information you gather.

The most critical aspect is not just creating positive relations between you and your students, but also between the students. And these positive relations are not an end in themselves but only when there are good relations and high trust are students likely to talk about what they do not know, talk about the help and new teaching they require, talk about misconceptions and errors—all the essence of great learners. If there are poor relationships in the class, students are hardly likely to confide that do not know and more likely to disengage. In addition to these aspects and considerations, it's also important to know where your students are in their learning journey. Too much time is spent in school on things that students have already learned. Nuthall (2006) showed about 40 percent to 50 percent of all content taught in classes the students know already—and this means they lack being challenged, lack the excitement of discovery, and see schools as places where they merely 'do' tasks. Assessing students allows you to develop lessons based on where your students are now, so that you and they can then advance to the next levels of skills and mastery. In fact, assessment information allows you to accelerate learning. To accelerate learning, we need to (Rollins, 2014)

➡ Identify skills that have yet to be learned

➡ Provide key aspects of knowledge in advance of instruction (sometimes called frontloading)

➜ Increase the relevance of students' learning

➜ Make connections with core academic learning goals

➜ Create active, fast-paced learning experiences

➜ Build students' confidence

Think about all the ways that assessment, when done well, could impact your ability to accelerate students' learning. That's the focus we hope for. Let's stop talking about gaps in learning and loss of learning and all those other ways that deficit thinking creeps into our minds and lowers our expectations. Instead, let's get to know our learners and their learning journey, and in doing so accelerate their progress.

There are a number of tools that you can use to identify where your learners are now. In Section 2, we focus on a wide range of ideas for collecting information about students. Many of these will work to determine students' current level of performance and allow to you align instruction accordingly.

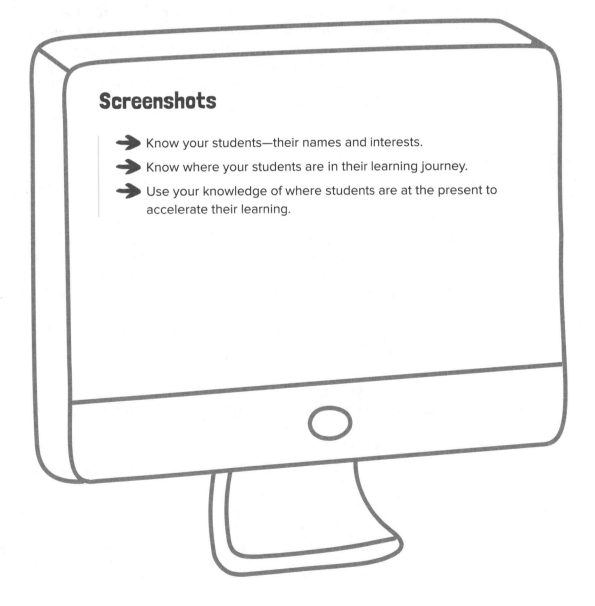

Screenshots

➜ Know your students—their names and interests.

➜ Know where your students are in their learning journey.

➜ Use your knowledge of where students are at the present to accelerate their learning.

ASSESSMENT COOKIE 4: ASSESS THAT WHICH HAS BEEN TAUGHT AND TEACH BASED ON THE STANDARDS

AN ASSESSMENT TOOL SHOULD NEVER BE CHOSEN BEFORE WE ENGAGE IN A DISCOVERY PROCESS ABOUT OUR LEARNERS.

You cannot design a good assessment without knowing your students as well as knowing what your students are learning. While this may seem like an obvious statement, it seems that when we engaged in pandemic teaching, we were caught up in the tools of assessment rather than the reasons for assessment. Think back to when the world pivoted to online teaching: social media pages were flooded with tips, tricks, and tools that could be used to assess students. In that emergent situation, teachers were cornered into choosing tools that promised to yield high impact assessments of our students. The issue we find with this moving forward in distance learning is that an assessment tool should never be chosen before we engage in a discovery process about our learners, have made transparent to them the criteria of what success in the lesson(s) look like, and have a purpose to discover what has been our impact on their learning. This requires a solid understanding of who is behind the learning as well as the standards you are assessing. This approach in turn will allow for more effective assessment practices.

Claudia Tamayo practices the three student questions of teacher clarity with her students.

resources.corwin.com/ AssessmentPlaybook

Knowing the expected learning outcomes (standards) is just as important as knowing our learners as we engage in assessment development. The standards drive instruction as well as provide a guidepost for assessment practices. After all, it is the standards against which we measure students' levels of understanding. It's not fair to include things on assessments that students were not expected to learn. In other words, assessments should align with instructional experiences. Instructional experiences should align with learning expectations and success criteria. And learning intentions and success criteria should align with the standards. There is so much research evidence that communicating these standards, say through using rubrics, to your students early in the learning helps the learning so much—and when online, this is even more important as the rubrics can serve as mini-steps to clarify progress to the success criteria.

Teachers provide clarity of standards to students through learning intentions and success criteria. And then instructional experiences help students reach the success criteria. These success criteria are the bases of student assessment, whether that be teacher to student, student to student, or student to self. Figure 4 highlights the progression of clarity from standards to success criteria.

4   STANDARDS, LEARNING INTENTIONS, AND SUCCESS CRITERIA

Standards	The standards provide us with concise, written descriptions of what students are expected to know and be able to do at a specific stage of their education.
Learning Intentions	Learning intentions adapt the language of the standards into student friendly and manageable statements. Learning intentions are broken down from the standards into lesson-sized chunks. They are statements of what a student is expected to learn.
Success Criteria	Success criteria provide a means for students and teachers to measure progress. They serve to indicate what the intended destination of learning looks like. Success criteria are fundamental in making learning visible to both the teacher and the student.

Source: Adapted from Edglossary.org https://www.edglossary.org/learning-standards/ and Fisher, D., Frey, N., Amador, O., & Assof, J. (2018). *The teacher clarity playbook, grades K–12: A hands-on guide to creating learning intentions and success criteria for organized, effective instruction*. Thousand Oaks, CA: Corwin.

Teaching and assessing based on the standards should occur irrespective of face-to-face, blended, or distance learning environment. As you build assessments through the lens of teacher clarity, consider the following three student questions:

1. What am I learning? (Learning Intentions)
2. Why am I learning it? (Relevance)
3. How will I know I have learned it? (Success Criteria)

Students should know the answers to these questions regardless of where they find themselves in their learning. By using these questions to guide our practice and our assessment, our students will have a better understanding of what is expected of them as well as what is required for success.

istock/valentinrussanov

Assessments should align with the content that has been taught.

istock/lakshmiprasad S

Instructional experiences should align with learning expectations and success criteria.

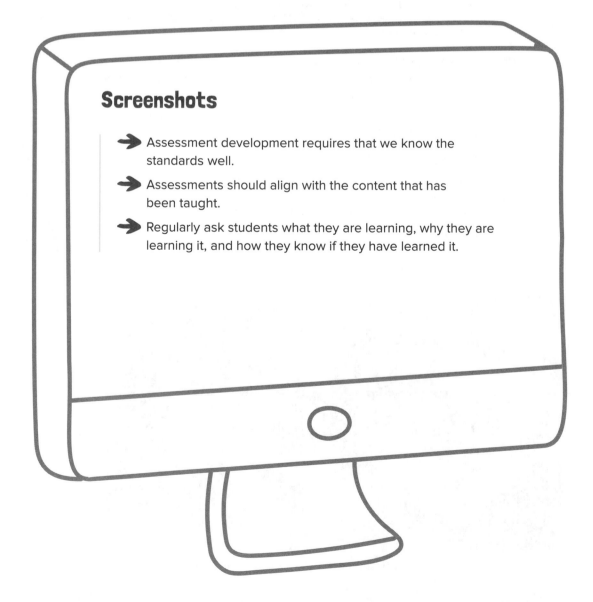

Screenshots

➡ Assessment development requires that we know the standards well.

➡ Assessments should align with the content that has been taught.

➡ Regularly ask students what they are learning, why they are learning it, and how they know if they have learned it.

ASSESSMENT COOKIE 5: STUDENTS DESERVE TO KNOW WHAT THEY SHOULD BE LEARNING

As mentioned previously, learning intentions are created based upon the standards we wish to teach and assess. Their purpose is to indicate to the student what they are learning that day. Good learning intentions that are aligned with standards invite students into learning. Further, they allow them to establish goals for their own learning. Learning intentions do not need to be shared at the outset of the lesson, but at some point, students should know what they are expected to learn.

There are several aspects that are valuable when creating learning intentions. The reason we focus on them in a book on assessment relates to their value in allowing teachers to choose the size and type of the tool to be used. In other words, the learning intention (and success criteria) guide the selection of the tools used to determine students' understanding and mastery. Without learning intentions, school can become a list of tasks to complete. In that case, the assessments are divorced from the learning and students often experience a "gotcha" feeling because they were not sure what they were supposed to learn, and the assessments feel like a trap. Figure 5 includes a number of considerations for creating learning intentions.

> WITHOUT LEARNING INTENTIONS, SCHOOL CAN BECOME A LIST OF TASKS TO COMPLETE.

5 LEARNING INTENTIONS CHECKLIST

Learning Intentions **should**	Learning Intentions **should not**
Be written in language that students understand	Restate the standard or objective
Be written in first person (student perspective)	Be written in third person (teacher perspective)
Include key concepts or vocabulary	Include a strategy (what the students are doing)
Include what the students are learning	Include a measure of assessment Focus only on the tasks to be completed

There are many ways to write learning intentions, and often teachers get bogged down in the details of how to write a perfect learning intention. As a matter of fact, writing any learning intention is fundamentally better than not including a learning intention at all. We recognize there is a spectrum of experiences and expertise with learning intentions. We encourage you to just start and not compare yourself with others. Think about the three clarity questions from the last cookie and try to help students answer the first question: *What am I learning today?* When students are clear about what they are learning, they are more likely to be engaged. As you grapple with writing learning intentions, you will come across multiple ways to write them. In many ways, the style of learning intention does not matter. What does matter is whether they follow the parameters mentioned above. In our examples, you will notice that we use the stems *I am learning . . .* and *We are learning . . .* This is simply a stylistic choice; however, if you are new to learning intentions, we do suggest that you choose one style and stick with it for consistency.

Analyzing standards to create learning intentions may seem daunting, however we hope the following will help provide clarity on learning intentions and their relationship to the standards. As you review your standards, please consider the following:

➡ Standards are often convoluted and most require multiple daily learning intentions.

➡ Learning intentions can provide the "why" to the standard. It helps to include the words "so that" at the end of the standard to help create learning intentions.

➡ Standards may include complex verbs or skills which may need to be broken down into multiple learning intentions.

Figure 6 includes examples of standards and learning intentions for your consideration.

6   EXAMPLES OF STANDARDS AND LEARNING INTENTIONS

Standard	Learning Intention
Grade 2 ELA Student applies knowledge of long and short vowel sounds to read unfamiliar words in context.	I am learning to identify short vowel sounds to help me read new words. I am learning to identify long vowel sounds to help me read new words.
Grade 3 Math Demonstrate an understanding of addition and subtraction of numbers with answers to 1000 (limited to 1-, 2- and 3-digit numerals), concretely, pictorially and symbolically by • Using personal strategies for adding and subtracting with and without the support of manipulatives • Creating and solving problems in context that involve addition and subtraction of numbers	We are learning to use models and personal strategies to add three-digit numbers. We are learning to use models and personal strategies to subtract three-digit numbers. We are learning to select and use appropriate strategies to accurately create and solve word problems involving addition. We are learning to select and use appropriate strategies to accurately create and solve word problems involving subtraction.

Source: ©Alberta Education. *Programs of Study; English Language Arts K–9: Use Strategies and Cues.* Edmonton, AB. 2000. p. 26. https://education.alberta.ca/media/160360/ela-pos-k-9.pdf ©Alberta Education. *Programs of Study; Mathematics Kindergarten to Grade 9: Number.* Edmonton, AB. 2016. p. 20. https://education.alberta.ca/media/3115252/2016_k_to_9_math_pos.pdf

 online resources   Available for download at **resources.corwin.com/AssessmentPlaybook**

istock/fbxx

As you grapple with writing learning intentions, you will come across multiple ways to write them.

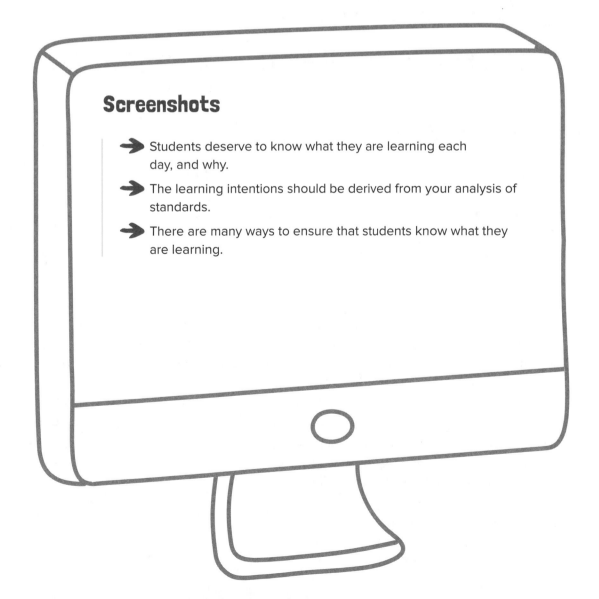

Screenshots

➡ Students deserve to know what they are learning each day, and why.

➡ The learning intentions should be derived from your analysis of standards.

➡ There are many ways to ensure that students know what they are learning.

ASSESSMENT COOKIE 6: KNOWING YOUR DESTINATION HELPS

Learning intentions do not exist in isolation. They need success criteria so our students can be aware of the third clarity question: *How will I know I have learned it?* The *it* being, of course, the learning intention. More specifically, success criteria specify for the students the necessary evidence they will need to produce to show they have achieved the learning intention. If success criteria are crafted carefully and with purpose, they can become the foundation of our assessments.

In fact, developing success criteria is necessary in the creation of assessment tasks and tools. When you know what success looks like, you can identify the various ways that students can demonstrate that success. When students know what success looks like, they are more likely to allocate resources (such as time and attention) to accomplishing the learning.

7 SUCCESS CRITERIA CHECKLIST

Success Criteria **should**	Success Criteria **should not**
Encourage students to show what they know	Be instructions or directions
Specify for students the evidence they will need to produce	Restrict the way students are demonstrating their learning
Deconstruct the process of meeting the learning intention	Repeat or restate the standard
Be written in language students understand	Be written in teacher friendly language

Much like learning intentions, teachers can get overwhelmed with creating the perfect success criteria statements. The truth is, by engaging and experimenting with success criteria we are already moving our students into the right direction when it comes to assessment. In our examples, you will notice that we use the stems *I can*… and *We can*… This is simply a stylistic choice, however if you are new to writing success criteria, we do suggest that you choose one style and stick with it for consistency. There are many other ways to ensure that students know what success looks like, such as rubrics, exemplars, and teacher modeling (Almarode, Fisher, Frey, & Thunder, 2021). As long as success criteria exist as an extension of learning intentions, we are practicing aspects of *clarity*.

It is important to note learning intentions often require multiple success criteria. The more intricate the learning intention, the more cues we will need to give our students in order for them to know they are successful. As we begin to develop success criteria, we should make the following considerations:

> ➡ Success criteria are used to provide a benchmark of success for the learning intention, and in some cases one learning intention will require multiple benchmarks.

➔ Success criteria can build in complexity as students move toward mastery.

➔ Success criteria should be built with the intention that students can use them to engage in metacognition.

Success criteria can be about the surface or "knowing that" part of the lesson (the needed subject vocabulary, the facts and ideas, the knowledge), and about the deep or "knowing how" part of the lesson (the conceptual understanding, the relations between ideas, the transfer to new situations). Often it is advisable to make both transparent to students, as quite often they think (despite what we say) that what is to be assessed are mainly the facts and knowledge. (Often, it is worth having two assessment questions, one about the "knowing that" and one about the "knowing how," and tell the students which is which, and show them you value both). Figure 8 includes examples of learning intentions and success criteria for your consideration. For more guidance and practice with learning intentions and success criteria, we suggest referring to *The Teacher Clarity Playbook*.

8 EXAMPLES OF LEARNING INTENTIONS AND SUCCESS CRITERIA

Standard/Learning Intention	Success Criteria
Mathematics 9 **Standard:** Model and solve problems, using linear equations of various forms. **Learning Intention:** I am learning to solve linear equations.	I can solve two-step equations. I can isolate the variable in the equation. I can explain the process of solving an equation. I can apply the distributive property. I can change an equation into a function. I can explain how the solution I arrived at relates to the function notation.
Social Studies 9 **Standard:** Examine the structure of Canada's federal political system by exploring and reflecting upon the following question: What is the relationship between the executive, legislative, and judicial branches of Canada's federal political system? **Learning Intention:** We are learning about the balance of powers among the three branches of government in Canada.	We can name the three branches of government. We can describe the primary function of each branch of government. We can compare and contrast each of their functions. We can describe the limitations of each branch of government. We can apply these limitations to the balance of power.

Source: ©Alberta Education. *Programs of Study; Mathematics Kindergarten to Grade 9: Patterns and Relations*. Edmonton, AB. 2016. p. 75. https://education.alberta.ca/media/3115252/2016_k_to_9_math_pos.pdf; ©Alberta Education. *Programs of Study; Social Studies Kindergarten to Grade 12: Issues for Canadians: Governance and Rights*. Edmonton. AB. 2007. p. 15. https://education.alberta.ca/media/160202/program-of-study-grade-9.pdf

 Available for download at **resources.corwin.com/AssessmentPlaybook**

Coming Full Circle: Standards, Learning Intentions, and Success Criteria

When combined, standards, learning intentions, and success criteria can help students navigate their way through learning. And they allow for the thoughtful creation of assessment tasks. Consider the metaphor of climbing a mountain. If the peak of the mountain acts as the standard and our students are at the bottom of this mountain, they will require guidance to the top. When hiking, the clearer and more visible the path, the safer the hiker is. This is no different in learning. A clear learning intention provides a way to the top. Learning intentions become the path in which students must navigate. Now the path to the top of a mountain is not easy, but as we get closer to the top there are markers of success which guide us in the right direction. Usually there are trail markers, signs, and indicators of distance remaining on a hike. Success criteria provides these markers for the learners as they navigate the path of their learning.

Naturally, students will require feedback as they move from one marker of success to the next and that is where it is fundamental that we engage in quality assessment. By moving through markers of success, hikers eventually make it to the top of the mountain and our students will make their way to the standard. Figure 9 provides a visual of the flow from standards to assessment.

9 **MOVING FROM STANDARDS TO ASSESSMENT**

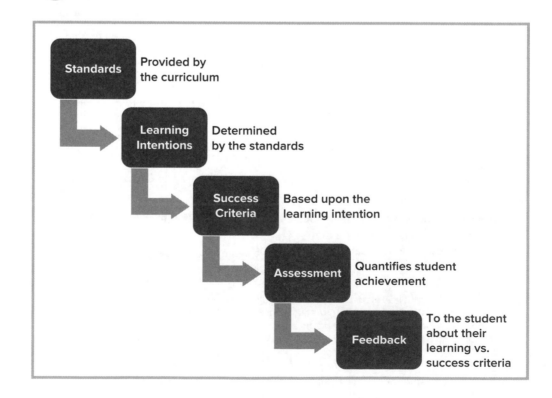

istock/RichLegg

Naturally, students will require feedback as they move from one marker of success to the next.

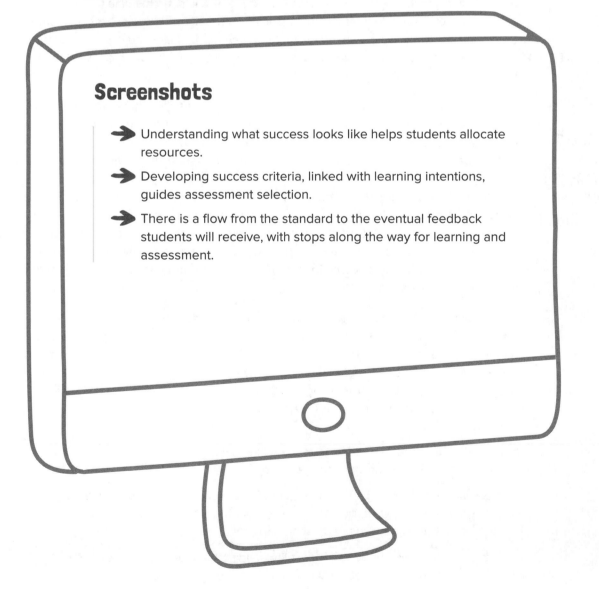

Screenshots

→ Understanding what success looks like helps students allocate resources.

→ Developing success criteria, linked with learning intentions, guides assessment selection.

→ There is a flow from the standard to the eventual feedback students will receive, with stops along the way for learning and assessment.

ASSESSMENT COOKIE 7: EVERYTHING IS SEARCHABLE, SO PLAN ACCORDINGLY

Many of the assessments given to students in physical school are under lock and key, meaning students are required to complete these in solitude with no possibility of an open book test. Many of our state and provincial exams are of this nature, so teachers want to mimic these types of assessments. These types of assessments are often seen as difficult, but we must reflect on whether they are rigorous.

Consider this. How might your assessments change should you remove the lock-and-key parameters mentioned above? If in reflection you found yourself wondering whether students would cheat, ask someone else for the answer, or simply just do an internet search, there is a possibility that that assessment lacks complexity, and thus is not rigorous. A multiple-choice exam in which students can search online for the correct answers is not a suitable assessment in distance learning and thus our task becomes determining what assessments are suitable in both authenticity and rigor in regard to student learning. Creating assessments that are rigorous and relevant to student learning is challenging, but important.

Remember that nearly everything can be researched online. Teachers are tasked with navigating through learning experiences and assessments knowing full well that students have access to the internet and that access can provide them answers to many of the questions asked on assessments. In order to keep students engaged in their learning and focused on meaningful assessment and evaluation, we must reconsider how to create assessments that require students to do more than simply find an answer. Although noted as a challenge, we can also look at this as an opportunity for us to reevaluate our assessment practices to ensure our students are receiving an evaluation that is fair, focused, and equitable. In doing so, we can hopefully eliminate opportunities for our students to search for answers via the internet and rather engage them in high-impact assessment.

How about this as a way to think about some of the assessment tasks you give: Can Siri or Alexa answer the question? If so, you may want to expand the types of assessments students are asked to complete. But before you throw out all those items, a quick review of the phases of learning is in order. Learning starts at the surface and progresses through transfer (see Figure 10). We think of these phases as follows (for more information see Fisher, Frey, & Hattie, 2016):

> **A MULTIPLE-CHOICE EXAM IN WHICH STUDENTS CAN SEARCH ONLINE FOR THE CORRECT ANSWERS IS NOT A SUITABLE ASSESSMENT IN DISTANCE LEARNING.**

- ➡ **Surface learning:** The foundational and introductory skills and concepts that students need to learn.
- ➡ **Deep learning:** The ability to identify the connections and relationships between various skills and concepts that have been learned. In deep learning, students develop schema.
- ➡ **Transfer of learning:** The ability to apply learning to new situations, to self-regulate learning, and to identify new learning opportunities.

10 PHASES OF LEARNING

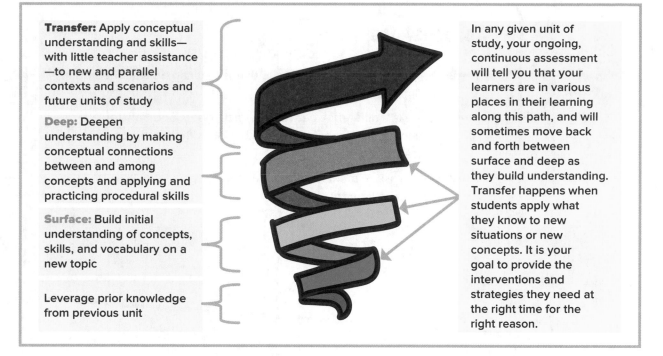

Transfer: Apply conceptual understanding and skills—with little teacher assistance—to new and parallel contexts and scenarios and future units of study

Deep: Deepen understanding by making conceptual connections between and among concepts and applying and practicing procedural skills

Surface: Build initial understanding of concepts, skills, and vocabulary on a new topic

Leverage prior knowledge from previous unit

In any given unit of study, your ongoing, continuous assessment will tell you that your learners are in various places in their learning along this path, and will sometimes move back and forth between surface and deep as they build understanding. Transfer happens when students apply what they know to new situations or new concepts. It is your goal to provide the interventions and strategies they need at the right time for the right reason.

Source: Hattie, J., Fisher, D., Frey, N., Gojak, L. M., Moore, S. D., & Mellman, W. (2016). *Visible learning for mathematics, grades K–12: What works best to optimize student learning.* Thousand Oaks, CA: Corwin.

Of course, assessments can be developed at any phase of learning. Google, Siri, and Alexa probably know the answers to many of the surface learning questions and tasks. But as learning progresses through deep and transfer, it's harder for students to simply ask their technology for the answer. Thus, our assessments need to scale from surface to deep to transfer. And assessment should include tasks that require students to search the internet and *then use that information for something else.* Teaching students how to access and assess the credibility of the information available digitally is an important skill.

istock/zoranm

Assessment should include tasks that require students to search the internet and then use that information for something else.

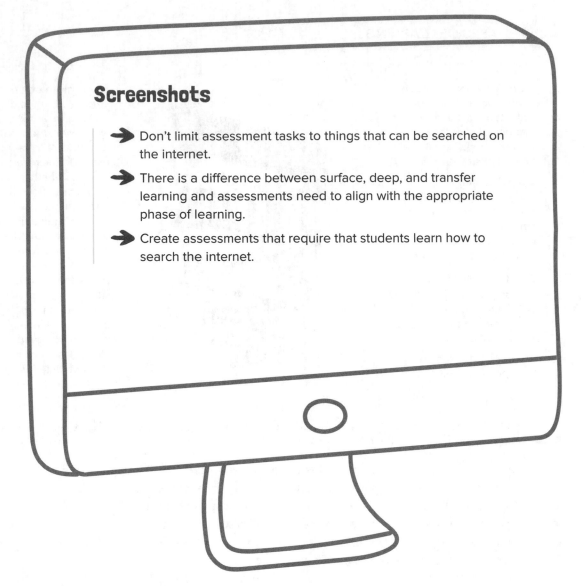

Screenshots

➡ Don't limit assessment tasks to things that can be searched on the internet.

➡ There is a difference between surface, deep, and transfer learning and assessments need to align with the appropriate phase of learning.

➡ Create assessments that require that students learn how to search the internet.

ASSESSMENT COOKIE 8: PARENTS WANT TO HELP AND SOMETIMES IT'S PROBLEMATIC

Parents can cause an unintended challenge related to assessment in the distance learning environment. Let us be clear before moving forward, sometimes a lot of the success of distance learning classrooms can be attributed to parental efforts. They can act as a fundamental component and liaison between student and teacher, especially at the younger grades. Parents are essential to the education of the student when it comes to setting up a home environment for learning and although they are well intended there are times when parents can get in the way of their child's learning. Let us first examine this using this example from a physical classroom.

> It is Sunday morning and at the breakfast table Mrs. Sharp asks her eight-year-old daughter, Sam, about the upcoming school week. When reminded about her homework, Sam gasps and reminds her mom that her science fair project is due that week. Immediately the Sharps jump into the car and head to the nearest craft store to buy supplies for the project. For the rest of the day, the family helps Sam with the creation of her science fair project. Thankfully, due to a family effort, the science project is completed, and Sam receives an A.

After reading this, take a guess as to who did the bulk of the project? If you guessed Sam's parents, there is a good chance you are correct. Although the Smith family meant well in their assistance of the science project, this assessment does not reflect what Sam knows about science.

We have noticed similarities in distance learning. On occasion when parents are learning alongside their children, there tends to be an overindulgence of support. Parents want their children to do well in school and on assessments which sometimes means they provide answers or deliberate coaching (even overhelping) for their children. We have even heard cases where parents tend to shout out the answers to questions during group or class discussions! We're not playing Jeopardy in the living room; we're trying to learn (recognizing the fact that Jeopardy is about creating questions, not answers).

Although we are happy that parents are excited and engaged in their child's learning, we must be cognizant of the fact that on occasion parents will get in the way of their child's learning. When it comes to assessments, parents can impact the validity of student evaluation should they get over involved, and in some cases, even complete tasks that were assigned to their child. This creates another layer of challenges for teachers who wish to engage in high quality assessments in distance learning.

As mentioned earlier, assessment is difficult because it is important. Rigorous, equitable and rich assessments are even more difficult to create because, well, they are even more important. Regardless of learning environment, our students deserve assessments that allow them to demonstrate their understanding with the utmost fidelity. It's helpful to explain this to family members. As we say,

> Please allow your child to struggle. Productive struggle is good for their brains. It's one of the ways we all learn. Please do not tell your child the answers or do the work for them—it is more about working to the answer than the answer itself. On practice and application tasks, you can provide all the hints you want but it is OK to let them do the work their way. If your child struggles too much, teach your child to talk to the teacher about this. On assessments, please allow your child some privacy to make mistakes so that the teacher knows what to do next. Remember, if your child gets everything right, the work was too easy.

It seems that there is a fairly significant need to help parents understand how to help children and their teachers. If not, the assessment data we collect may not be worth the storage it takes on your computer. We need good, accurate information so that we can make sound instructional decisions. In distance and blended learning, this means educating family members as well.

istock/damircudic

Parents can cause an unintended challenge related to assessment in the distance learning environment.

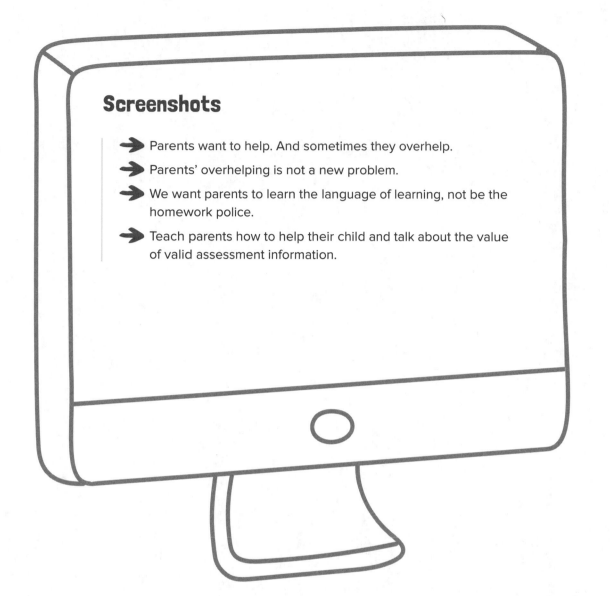

Screenshots

➤ Parents want to help. And sometimes they overhelp.

➤ Parents' overhelping is not a new problem.

➤ We want parents to learn the language of learning, not be the homework police.

➤ Teach parents how to help their child and talk about the value of valid assessment information.

2 THE PLAYLISTS

Like most of you, we each have our favorite songs assembled into playlists on our devices. In a mellow mood? You've probably got one for that. Energizing music to exercise to? Likely the songs on that playlist are different from the ones on the first one. Arguably the best feature is the shuffle function, which allows you to create a different order each time.

We've titled this section The Playlists because we want to encourage you to have a repertoire of assessment processes that match your purpose. Like your music or video playlist, there is no prescribed order. You can play these items over and over. Each assessment playlist achieves a particular purpose, an acknowledgment that no single assessment could ever do everything you need. Like your music playlists, you select them based on what you want to accomplish. We invite you to add these to your growing distance learning playlist.

In this section:

- ☐ ASSESSMENT THROUGH UNIVERSAL RESPONSE
- ☐ TEACH-BACK
- ☐ ASSESSMENT THROUGH COMPOSING
- ☐ SELF- AND PEER ASSESSMENT

PLAYLIST 1: ASSESSMENT THROUGH UNIVERSAL RESPONSE

"On the count of three . . . one, two, three, SEND!" High school mathematics teacher Morgan Kennedy has just posed a question to her students about properties of logarithms for an equation she has shared using the whiteboard feature in her virtual classroom. The students have been learning about product property, power property, and quotient property in their distance learning Math 3 course. "These concepts can be confusing when they're first learning about them, and we spend quite a bit of time differentiating the characteristics of each," the teacher later explained. However, Ms. Kennedy also knows that her more hesitant students will often wait a few seconds for others to respond in the chat, and then provide a similar answer once they've seen how others reply. "I've learned that I can't always get an accurate gauge on who knows something and who doesn't when I would ask a question like that." Her chat is still an active one, but when she needs to check for understanding she uses a technique called a Waterfall Chat. After posing the question, she asks her students to type their answer but wait for the signal to submit. The result is a flood of replies that come in at once. "I get much better feedback about who knows something and who doesn't," said the teacher. She also needs a record, so she saves the chat at the end of the class so she can analyze it further. "I can zero in on the specific students that are having more difficulty and set up some small group time with them for reteaching."

Universal Response

Universal responses are those techniques used by the teacher to allow for simultaneous replies from every member of the group, rather than isolated answers. A goal of universal response is to solicit answers from all the students in order to check for understanding and obtain a sense of whether the instruction is sticking or not. In other words, it is assessment *for* learning. The benefits of universal response opportunities are twofold. First, they provide you a chance to get a quick read on student understanding in real time. The second benefit is that these micro-assessments prompt learners to consider their own knowledge in the moment. The cognitive dissonance that comes from finding out that the reply was incorrect can open a dialogue as they ask questions and seek clarification. In other words, it shifts learning from a passive to an active endeavor.

Examples of universal response abound in face-to-face classrooms. Teachers routinely use response cards and student whiteboards to gain a sense of what each child can do. Another example is when students use hand signals, such as a fist-to-five signaling their agreement about a statement, or a thumbs up/thumbs down response for dichotomous questions, such as yes/no or true/false. These and other universal response techniques are easily adapted to a distance learning environment and are featured in this playlist. Consider these to be an initial way of being able to assess your students in the moment in order to make instructional adjustments.

Rehearsal and Retrieval as a Function of Learning

Are you old enough to recall when we used to memorize other people's phone numbers? With the advent of smartphones that feature contact lists and a favorites function for frequently called numbers, most of us would be hard-pressed to write down the phone numbers of our siblings, parents, and best friends. It turns out that knowing those numbers is solely a function of using them daily or weekly. We don't know them because we don't engage in rehearsal and retrieval. Without rehearsal and retrieval, we never leave a "memory trace" in our brains (Roediger & Karpicke, 2006). Think of a memory trace like the tire tracks left behind on a sandy surface. We know that a vehicle traveled through the area because we can see the track marks. More importantly, we could follow the path and find the vehicle more quickly because of the trail. Your memory works like that, too. The clearer the path, the easier and quicker it is to locate information. And the path gets clearer with rehearsal. The more times you need to find that information, the more permanent the information becomes. When you check for understanding, you're creating another opportunity for the learner to have to retrieve knowledge.

Wait Time as a Function of Learning

Ms. Kennedy's Waterfall technique in the opening scenario utilizes another important concept for learning: wait time or think time as we consider it in distance learning. Students benefit from time to be able to process a question and formulate an answer. Somewhere between three and ten seconds is recommended for wait time, with longer wait times especially beneficial for English learners. Unfortunately, wait time in classroom settings is often one second or less, allowing virtually no one the chance to think (Gambrell, 1983).

The need for wait time in distance learning is increased in part due to small transmission delays. Keep in mind that just because you heard yourself saying something doesn't mean your students heard it in that moment. You know those delays you hear on a broadcast when one journalist is speaking to another from the other side of the world? Although not quite as long, they exist. There are other delays inherent to a virtual environment. If you're asking students to respond in writing, they need time to do so. If they are responding verbally, they need time to unmute their microphone. The silence that follows a question can feel like an eternity; it's not. Between the need to cognitively process, the audio signal delay, and the actions required to respond, those silences are an indication of the need for increased wait time, not more teacher talk.

Pacing and Feedback as Functions of Learning

Another dimension of universal responding is that it can quicken the pace of learning through increased opportunities to answer questions. Although none of us subscribes to a strictly behavioral theory of engagement, more frequent interactions between teacher and students increase the amount of on-task time as they are repeatedly reengaged. A useful rule of thumb is to alternate about ten minutes or so of teacher talk with one or two universal response questions.

In terms of assessment, the use of universal responses provides the teacher with more feedback opportunities, compared to individual responses (Haydon, Marsicano, & Scott, 2013). For instance, a class of twenty-five who universally respond to a question allows the teacher a way to give feedback to twenty-five students. Questions that are addressed to only one student mean that twenty-four others did not benefit from a feedback opportunity. This is not to say that questions answered by individuals are not valuable. However, in practice the majority of individual questions are answered by a handful of students, with universal responses occurring much more rarely, especially beyond the primary grades. Distance learning is emerging as a renewed chance to add universal responses to the assessment repertoire.

Hand Signals

"I'm going to ask a question next. Show me a thumbs up if you agree and, if you don't, show me a thumbs down." Kindergarten teacher Allen Richards is in the middle of an interactive read aloud with his students in his virtual classroom. They're reading *A Bike Like Sergio's* (Boelts, 2016) and talking about the ethical dilemma faced by Ruben, who longs for a new bicycle like his friend. Ruben finds a $100 bill and starts imagining the ways he might spend it, including helping his mother to pay for groceries. He soon realizes who it belongs to and wrestles with the dilemma of whether to return it or not. Mr. Richards asks, "If you were Ruben's friend, would you tell him to return it? After all, he has some ideas about how he could use it." The teacher scans the screen as his students show him their opinion and selects two students with differing opinions to share their thoughts.

Even the youngest learners can use hand signals to indicate their responses. Most of them are pretty intuitive. The most basic is the thumbs up/thumbs down signal for dichotomous choices. Mr. Richards regularly uses this universal response technique to find out where his students are in their thinking, "like a temperature check," he said. More complex questions can be answered using Fist to Five. Students use the correct number of fingers to indicate their level of agreement or disagreement with a particular statement.

→ **Fist**: This topic is new to me and I need more information before I make a choice.

→ **One finger**: I completely disagree with this statement and can offer several reasons to support my position.

→ **Two fingers**: I disagree with this statement and can offer one reason to support my position.

→ **Three fingers**: I am unsure of where I stand on this issue and am interested in hearing from others.

→ **Four fingers**: I agree with this statement and can offer one reason to support my position.

→ **Five fingers**: I completely agree with this statement and can offer several reasons to support my position.

Eighth-grade history teacher Julia Molina uses fist-to-five as a prelude to her breakout rooms:

I'll pose a meaty statement for them to consider, like "America is the land of opportunity." We're currently discussing inequities that can be traced back to the founding of this country. Our first small group discussions are in breakout rooms with similarly minded peers. Students who choose a 3 divide their time between the "disagree" and "agree" groups to form an opinion. If there are any students who show a fist, I keep them in the main room with me to clarify or fill in knowledge gaps. Everybody will then come back to the main room for our first whole-class discussion. Later, I'll remix them so the rooms represent the span of opinions. Fist-to-five lets me assess where they are so I can group and regroup them.

Ms. Molina noted that in her face-to-face classroom she would use opinion corners to accomplish a similar arrangement. "They can't physically move around the room, but I can group them virtually." She started using this approach when her school began conducting distance learning, and she plans to keep doing so when students are together. "I realize now that there were lots of students who followed their friends to a corner and didn't really bother to form an opinion. This lets me see what their opinion really is."

Response Cards

Another face-to-face classroom technique that is readily adaptable to a virtual setting is response cards. These can be used in a variety of formats and include signs or other items that are held up simultaneously to answer a question. They may be preprinted or students may use whiteboards to write their answers. A meta-analysis of eighteen studies on the use of preprinted and write-on response cards showed that they were associated with higher achievement on tests and quizzes, higher levels of participation, and lower levels of disruptive behavior, compared to individual hand raising to answer a question (Randolph, 2007).

There are some benefits and challenges to using response cards in distance learning. In addition to the associated feedback that accompanies increased opportunities to respond, older students who might otherwise perceive response cards as being too juvenile for them in a face-to-face classroom are more likely to use them in a virtual space. "My kids understand that using a response card helps me as a teacher when all I can see of them are these small boxes in a grid on my screen," remarked biology teacher Jeremy Zhang. However, a challenge is that, like hand signals, cameras need to be on. "That's an ongoing conversation I have with some students," said the teacher. "There are a lot of sensitivities to take into account. In those cases, I ask them to turn on their camera momentarily, or respond to me through a private message."

Third-grade teacher Kendra Benson's school included response cards with the supplies distributed by the school. In addition to a laptop, paper, scissors, a ruler, pencils and crayons, her students received the following:

➡ A used CD or DVD case that showed red paper on one side and green on the other

➡ A small whiteboard with dry erase markers and a cloth for wiping

➡ Preprinted cards held together on a ring so that students can easily find them:

  • Arithmetic symbols

  • The letters *A–D* for multiple-choice questions

  • The numbers 1–4 for self-assessments

  • A true/false card

➡ Preprinted cards to solicit teacher response, including ones that reads "help, please," "repeat, please," and another with a question mark on it.

"These response cards have been a lifesaver for me," said Ms. Benson. "Knowing that students have them has prompted me to use them more. They can also signal to me when they need something, which gives me some in-the-moment feedback."

Response boards are particularly effective for monitoring what is written. Each student has a small whiteboard and washable board marker at their disposal. Throughout the lesson, the teacher instructs students to write answers to questions and hold up their response boards. This provides an opportunity to assess the knowledge of the class and clear up misunderstandings. First-grade teacher Noelle Lawson, a teacher at the same school, has made use of the student whiteboards. "I need to be able to monitor their handwriting and composition skills," said Ms. Lawson. She uses the whiteboards nearly every day in small group and whole class synchronous sessions. "I've always had them write during small-group guided instruction. They might be writing vocabulary words or composing sentences in response to a reading. Now that we're in distance learning, I'm using the same practice, but now they hold it up to the camera so I can observe their work," she said.

Her colleague Juanita Ross teaches seventh-grade math. Even though her students received the whiteboards at the beginning of the year, she initially didn't use them. "I didn't use them in my physical classroom, so it really wasn't something I was familiar

The two videos below show students using whiteboards:

Students use whiteboards to practice math problems.

Students use whiteboards to practice phonics.

resources.corwin.com/ AssessmentPlaybook

with." However, after the first week, she realized that asking her students to write on paper and hold it up to the laptop camera didn't work. "I couldn't read what they had written with a pencil or a pen," said Ms. Ross. "The whiteboard and marker make for a sturdier and brighter surface. The marker is thicker than a pencil so I can see their equations and give them feedback."

Polling

Teachers have long solicited feedback from students in the form of polls. Whether voting on the picture book that will be read aloud after lunch, co-constructing class-room norms, or selecting representatives for student government, these activities let teachers know the opinions of their students. However, to poll students about answers to questions was a cumbersome process and therefore rarely done. Technology advances in the last decade have made polling much easier to get immediate feedback and detect misconceptions. Commercial and open source programs such as Kahoot and Poll Everywhere, as well as built-in polling features in many learning management systems (LMS) have rapidly increased the use of polling for assessment and learning.

Questions are constructed in advance by the teacher in the form of multiple-choice questions. Some polling features allow for open-response questions, too, which is even better. Sixth-grade social studies teacher Mariam Ohanian routinely uses open-response questions to gauge learning and solicit feedback from her students and sets the visualization display so that all the student responses are listed as a text wall. "We're currently studying early humans and it can be a difficult topic to engage eleven-year-olds in," she said. "There's lots of misconceptions about cave-men living with dinosaurs, and then there's those old *Flintstones* cartoons they find on YouTube," Ms. Ohanian chuckled. "I use polling throughout the session to ask them questions, like 'What's an example of this in modern life?' They can immediately see each other's responses and I can scan them quickly to build on their ideas. I can ask a follow up question of specific students, like saying 'Sean, that's a really interesting example. Tell us more.'"

Third-grade teacher Vanessa Franklin uses multiple-choice polling questions when she teaches math in her virtual classroom. Ms. Franklin provides a word problem and four possible solutions for her students to pick from, and their results are displayed in a bar chart. However, she doesn't reveal the correct answer yet. "After briefly explaining the results, I send them into breakout rooms with the direction to justify their choice and listen to the reasoning of others," said Ms. Franklin. "When they come back into the main room, they take the same poll question again." At that point, she reveals the correct response and asks students to explain why the other three choices couldn't be correct. "It's amazing how many more students choose correctly after spending a few minutes talking with their peers," she said.

Sometimes there are polling questions that stump a larger portion of the group, even after talking with peers. "That's my cue that I need to back up and do some re-teaching and clarifying before moving forward," said the teacher. "Knowing when to go faster and when to slow down has really helped me increase the precision of my teaching."

Ninth-grade English teacher Anthony Walsh uses the word cloud function to augment comprehension of complex texts. After their first silent reading of a passage, he invites his students to post any unfamiliar words or phrases they encountered. The relative size of the text in the word cloud gives him an indication of how widespread the confusion might be. "I don't want to spend too much time preteaching vocabulary when we're doing a close reading," Mr. Walsh explained. "I do want them to use their knowledge of structural and contextual clues to figure them out." Using the feedback provided through the word cloud responses, the English teacher then selects the words most commonly chosen to think aloud and model how he arrives at the meaning. "Then I turn it back over to them for a second silent reading, and we repeat the process again. There's usually a big decrease because students are applying similar problem-solving skills to resolve unfamiliar terms."

Assessment in distance learning is multifaceted, as we will continue to explore in upcoming playlist entries in this section. However, the regular use of universal response opportunities promotes active engagement and gives you a quick temperature check of the class as you make instructional decisions in the moment.

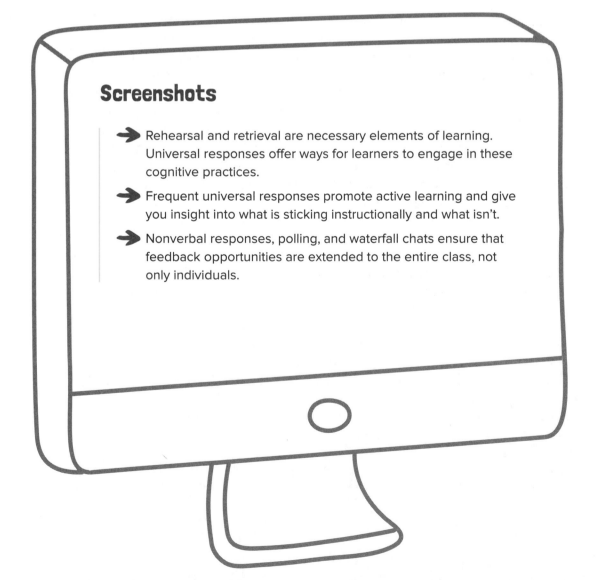

Screenshots

➡ Rehearsal and retrieval are necessary elements of learning. Universal responses offer ways for learners to engage in these cognitive practices.

➡ Frequent universal responses promote active learning and give you insight into what is sticking instructionally and what isn't.

➡ Nonverbal responses, polling, and waterfall chats ensure that feedback opportunities are extended to the entire class, not only individuals.

PLAYLIST 2: TEACH-BACK

"Thank you so much for watching how to compare numbers."

Second-grader Jazmine has just concluded her Flipgrid lesson on comparisons of six-digit numbers. She has been learning about place values in Sara Ortega's math class. As part of Ms. Ortega's assessment menu, the teacher asks her students to teach their own short lesson to explain a concept they are learning. Called "teach-back," these short student-developed lessons allow learners to construct their knowledge by teaching something they are learning. Jazmine uses a whiteboard to demonstrate how she determines which of the two is larger. She moves through each place value, until she arrives at the difference at the 10,000 place value. "5 and 3 are not equal," she asserts, and then explains how she uses the < sign (she calls it an alligator) in her mathematical equation. You can watch Jazmine's video to see her in action.

Jazmine uses Flipgrid to teach-back by showing how to compare large numbers.

Teach-back offers multiple benefits. First, it solidifies student knowledge. When students explain and demonstrate, they must go through the process of organizing their thinking. A crucial measure is that your students are clear that "the standard of knowing is the ability to explain *to* others, not understanding when explained *by* others" (Willingham, 2003). Explaining to others demonstrates that the student can become a teacher—the epitome of becoming a Visible Learner.

Students need opportunities to explain to others. When learning is shared with others in the class, peers profit from witnessing explanations that are coming from someone who is learning alongside them. Vygotsky proposed that peer-mediated learning promotes cognitive gains (1978). Learning is often a social act, as we learn in the company of other humans. Even in digital spaces, virtual contact with others is vital. The opportunity to speak or write can serve as a means to clarify one's own thinking about a topic. It allows students to think aloud, to demonstrate their self-explanations and self-questioning, to learn self-verbalization, and just as critically, to understand how others may have different strategies and language for attending to the same tasks and problems. How often have you experienced a heightened sense of your own knowledge even as you were in the process of explaining it to someone else? This restructuring of one's own thinking is called cognitive elaboration, and results when learners explain ideas to each other and discuss any gaps in their understanding (Chi, 2000).

A student practices reading by reading to his stuffed animal.

resources.corwin.com/ AssessmentPlaybook

Finally, teach-back is at its heart a form of assessment for you to gauge your students' learning by providing insights into their cognitive and metacognitive thinking. This is consistent with the student mindframes, which are habits and dispositions that accelerate learning. One of the mindframes is recognizing your learning and teaching others (Frey et al., 2018). This mindframe is a necessary component for transfer of learning, which is the application of skills and concepts to new and novel situations (Biggs, 1999).

Once a child has learned something, teaching it to someone else can assist in transfer or ownership of that learning. The effect size research is pretty clear about this. Peers tutoring each other benefit both. As French writer Joseph Joubert suggests, teaching something to someone else allows you to learn it twice. You can set up opportunities for your students to teach others—classmates, or perhaps even younger siblings. There's also an opportunity to teach others in the community, virtually and without the teacher present. It's even been shown that reading to a pet can boost reading skills (Wiseman et al., 2020).

Cognitive Task Analysis

How do you explain something to your students? It's more complex than just telling young people some facts and hoping for the best. Undoubtedly you have developed your teaching skills through professional learning, guided experiences, professional dialogue, and instructional coaching. Each of these dimensions has given you the opportunity to watch and engage with experts at their craft. Importantly, you didn't just watch them. If observation was all that was necessary, we could all be Olympic athletes or world-class musicians. You engaged in cognitive task analysis (CTA) to identify and understand the purposes, skills, mental demands, and actions they used to perform the complex task of effective teaching (Chi, Glaser, & Farr, 1988). You then put these into practice, refining your own skills through continued dialogue with others.

Students who teach-back use a form of cognitive task analysis to break down steps and organize their explanations. In this case, you're the expert they are analyzing. As with all of the assessment types we've discussed, students should know in advance how they will be assessed. When students know they will be teaching a skill or concept to someone else, they analyze differently. The audience is a key factor in this process. Knowing you'll be responsible for teaching someone else alerts you to the fact that you'll need to understand the nuances of how knowledge is built.

Class Teach-Back

There are times in the lives of nearly every teacher when we think to ourselves, "There's thirty-five of them and only one of me." That feeling can be even more heartfelt in a distance learning environment. But in truth, you have the potential thirty-five teaching assistants in your remote classroom. Make the most of this by empowering students to teach one another. In doing so, you also glean valuable assessment information about the progress of each child, including providing corrective feedback and reteaching when you see partial understandings or misconceptions emerge.

Middle school science teacher Jason Ning has been using teach-back in his classes for the first time this school year. "I have fewer instructional minutes with them than I had last year, so I want to make the most of the time," he said. "Teach-back to the class has increased the quality of the asynchronous part of my class, and I get to assess." He introduces the success criteria at the beginning of the unit and has them self-rank for expected difficulty (see Playlist 4 on self-assessment), a practice he has been using for several years. He expanded this to include a sign-up for each success criteria. "I've got between 31 and 34 kids per period," Mr. Ning explained. "Let's say I have 5 success criteria for a unit. Students sign up for the success criteria item they want to teach. I screen them to make sure they are correct and provide feedback to them before they teach it." When the teach-back submission is ready, Mr. Ning posts it on his class LMS.

Sometimes students have to revise their video submissions, which is a part of the assessment-for-learning element of the task. His intention with posting them, rather than just viewing them himself, is to support their study habits. "As we ramp up to the end-of-unit assessment, the students can access the teach-back submissions for each of the success criteria," said the science teacher. "These two-minute peer explanations augment the other study materials they have." Claire, a student in his class, echoed a similar sentiment. "We have a practice test in Mr. Ning's class like a week before the end [of the unit]," said the student (see Upgrade 2 for more information on practice tests). "That way I know what I still need to study. And one of the things I do is check out the teach-back videos for the success criteria I'm having trouble with." Because the teacher vets each teach-back before publicly posting it, Claire and the other students can trust that the information is correct. For Mr. Ning, "It's feeding two birds with one crumb," he said. "Students are getting additional peer supports for learning, and I get some valuable assessment data throughout the unit. It lets me interrupt misconceptions and monitor the progress of the class. All in all, it's a win-win." Mr. Ning's quality indicators checklist for students is in Figure 11.

11 QUALITY INDICATORS FOR TEACH-BACK

Directions: Plan your teach-back video submission in advance. Write your major talking points on a sticky note and post it near your computer camera so you can refer to them as you explain. You have two minutes, so you want to be concise and precise. Keep these quality indicators in mind.

- Begin by telling your audience what concept or skill you will be explaining.

- Refer to the specific success criteria you are referencing.

- Provide an explanation that is accurate.

- Make sure to explain your thinking, not just the factual knowledge. A good way to do this is to use a language frame for a concept such as, "I know this because . . ." If it is a skill, you can use a language frame such as, "I do this because . . ."

- Be sure to look at the camera, check your lighting and your audio quality.

- Play it back before submitting, using this checklist as a guide.

- When you submit your video file, please use this naming convention: [Last Name]_Success Criteria #_[Name of concept or skill].

Teach-Back to the Family

Teaching back is not limited to peers. In distance learning, students can also teach back to their family members. We are not suggesting that parents perform assessment tasks with or on their child, but rather that they become key figures in communicating information to us as teachers as well as audience members for their children's instruction. In order for this to occur, there are some important parameters.

1. Parents must be clear in the learning intentions and success criteria in their child's learning. This will help them understand the context for the experience.

2. Parents are NOT assessing their child, but rather become facilitators of assessment (e.g., helping their child as they self-assess, translating and transcribing single point rubrics for their child).

3. Parents can be involved in assignment submission to the teacher (e.g., taking photos of a product, submitting through a Google Classroom, emailing the teacher).

A student practices teach-back with his sister.

Mr. and Mrs. Hernandez were clear about how they approached this with their fifth grader at home. As Mr. Hernandez said, "At our school, they have Teach-Back Tuesday. That means every Tuesday, our son Antonio has to teach us things that he's learned. We try to video it so that his teacher can see it. It's become part of our family tradition and I ask him about what he will be teaching us every Tuesday morning."

When we talked with Antonio, he had a little different perspective. He said, "I give them problems first. If they do it right, then don't teach them. I only teach the ones that they get wrong. You don't gotta teach it if they already know it." Out of the mouth of babes! Imagine if we all took Antonio's advice and focused our instruction on things that our students needed to learn and cut out all of the minutes focused on things that they already knew. The potential is amazing.

A student practices teach-back with her baby brother.

Teach-back can occur across grade levels and subject areas. The key is to obtain information about the teach-back to see which parts of the lessons stuck and if there are any misconceptions or errors that need to be addressed. Sherry Clifford had her history students teach the content to their family members. The students made presentations, much more formal than she originally thought that they would, and conducted lessons with their families. They even had response opportunities to check for understanding. As Ms. Clifford watched these lessons, she noted that many of her students did not include information about roads and canals as they taught their families about the building of transportation networks. As she noted, "They seemed to all focus on the railroads. That's important, but there's more to that period of time that helped shape the nation. Seeing what they taught to their families helped me think about lessons that I needed to design so that they had a more complete understanding of this period in history."

Retelling to Teach Others

Sarah Ortega's class practices retelling by using the "hot seat" question.

resources.corwin.com/ AssessmentPlaybook

An interesting way to determine what students know and remember is to invite them to retell the information. When they have to produce the information in their own words, you'll get a sense of what stuck and if there are any misconceptions or errors. Retellings are not new and have been used to assess students for several decades (e.g., Morrow, 1985). There is evidence that retellings are useful for assessment; they also improve comprehension itself (e.g., Koskinen, Gambrell, Kapinus, & Heathington, 1988). The process is simple. Students are invited to retell what they remember. Teachers can use rubrics or checklists to guide students' retellings or simply invite them to explain what they remember. Two sample rubrics, for narrative and informational texts, are found in Figures 12 and 13. One challenge with retellings in the physical classroom is time. Often, teachers cannot have all students retell because they run out of time and class is over. In distance learning, students can video or audio record their retellings and teachers can use that information to plan future instruction. In addition to their use as assessment tools, they can be shared with other members of the class for additional learning opportunities.

12 NARRATIVE STORY RETELLING RUBRIC

Name: _____   Teacher: _____

Title of book: _____

Who read the story?   ☐ Teacher   ☐ Student

	Proficient—3	Adequate—2	Needs Attention—1
Character	Main and supporting characters and their characteristics identified. Examples given to describe characters.	Most main and supporting characters identified. Characteristics are less descriptive.	Characters essential to the story are overlooked. Few or no examples or descriptions of characteristics offered.
Setting	Setting is identified and described in detail using vivid vocabulary.	Setting is identified and description is accurate. Some detail included.	Setting is either not identified or identified incorrectly.
Problem	Central problem of the story is identified. Character motivations or potential solutions included.	Central problem is identified. Character motivations or potential solutions are not included.	Central problem is not dentified or is incorrectly identified.
Solution	Solution is identified. Retelling features connections to characteristics of characters. Student relates this to story's moral or theme.	Solution is identified but retelling does not include connection to moral or theme.	Solution is not identified or is incorrectly identified.
Plot	Sequence of story is told in correct order.	Sequence of story is told in nearly correct order, with one or two events out of sequence.	Sequence of story has three or more errors.

Script retelling in the box below, then score quality of the retelling.

	Character: _____
	Setting: _____
	Problem: _____
	Solution: _____
	Plot: _____
	TOTAL: _____

Source: Fisher, D., Frey, N., & Hattie, J. (2017). *Teaching literacy in the visible learning classroom, grades K–5.* Thousand Oaks, CA: Corwin.

online resources 🖰 Available for download at **resources.corwin.com/AssessmentPlaybook**

13 INFORMATIONAL TEXT RETELLING RUBRIC

Name: _____   Teacher: _____

Title of book: _____

Who read the story?   ☐ Teacher   ☐ Student

	Proficient—3	Adequate—2	Needs Attention—1
Main Ideas	Main ideas are identified. Examples are given to illustrate these ideas.	Most main ideas identified. Examples are less descriptive.	Main ideas essential to the text are overlooked. Few or no examples or descriptions of main ideas offered.
Supporting Details	Supporting details are clearly connected to the main ideas.	Supporting details are identified but are not told in association with main ideas.	Few or no supporting details offered.
Sequence	Sequence of retelling is accurate and reflects the order used by the author.	Sequence is similar to order in book, with some instances of "doubling back" during retelling.	Sequence is difficult to discern.
Accuracy	Facts are relayed accurately.	Retelling is mostly accurate, with few errors.	Retelling is inaccurate.
Inferences	Student makes connections within text (e.g., meaning of title, usefulness of information).	Student makes few associations between pieces of information in text.	Student makes no associations within text.

Script retelling in the box below, then score quality of the retelling.

	Main Ideas: _____
	Details: _____
	Sequence: _____
	Accuracy: _____
	Inferences: _____
	TOTAL: _____

Source: Fisher, D., Frey, N., & Hattie, J. (2017). *Teaching literacy in the visible learning classroom, grades K–5.* Thousand Oaks, CA: Corwin.

 Available for download at **resources.corwin.com/AssessmentPlaybook**

Retellings are not just for elementary students. Julia Madsen's high school English class is studying short stories. Over the course of several weeks, she has been noticing that some students are missing aspects of comprehension in the stories she has been assigning. "I am finding that many of my students are missing key themes from our short story unit, so I decided to allow students to try peer support." Ms. Madsen used the retelling strategy with her learners. She assigned each student a short story to read asynchronously, reminding students they would be retelling their story to a peer. She noted a rather immediate impact: "My students are asking more in-depth questions about the texts that I have assigned, which tells me that they are engaging with the material in a deeper way." Before assigning the texts to her students, Ms. Madsen made sure to model what retelling looked like as well as showing her students videos to ensure students were aware of how to apply this strategy.

A student practices retelling by sharing a book he read and answering questions about his reading.

Students were placed in breakout rooms where they were responsible for retelling their assigned short story to a peer. Once they completed this task, they self-assessed their comprehension of the story as well as their ability to engage in a conversation about the text, both of which were known via the learning intentions and success criteria for the assignment. When reflecting on this retelling process, Ms. Madsen noticed a shift in her students' behaviors.

"My students opened up about their experiences with the text and were more open to reading new ones. Many of them noticed they had to read the stories with more attention so they could retell them with fidelity."

As a result of their retelling assessment, students' understanding of complicated texts improved drastically and the love of learning English blossomed. Students who take ownership of their learning are more engaged in their assessment.

A student retells the story "As Fast as Words Can Fly."

Student-Created Podcasts

Social studies teacher Josh Luukkonen uses student-created podcasts as a means for students to teach back to the class and the world. A fan of podcasts himself, he leverages both families' and students' experiences to help teach his unit on immigration.

"Our school has a lot of immigrant students and I've been thinking wouldn't it be cool to document the stories of all of these different immigrants and make a sort of historical record of the people that came to our city in this small corner of time?"

Students in Mr. Luukkonen's ninth-grade social studies class must find an immigrant new to Canada and interview them about their experiences. The students are required to

A student retells the story "Gustavo, the Shy Ghost."

resources.corwin.com/AssessmentPlaybook

➜ Find out why the people came to Edmonton, Canada

➜ Ask about what life was like in their home country

➜ Ask about what they prefer about living in Canada

➜ Listen and learn from these stories

"Most of the students interview their parents, but others interview neighbors, cousins—I even had a student interview the school custodian—and in season two of the podcast I

Josh Luukkonen describes the process of creating a podcast with his students.

resources.corwin.com/ AssessmentPlaybook

was even interviewed, because I became a Canadian citizen in 2019. We have had easy immigration stories, stories of hardship and near death and even stories of refugees escaping some terrible situations in their home countries," said Mr. Luukkonen.

The students are responsible for almost all aspects of the podcast, from finding interview subjects and recording them to creating the logo for the podcast. Mr. Luukkonen even said that he had other students in the school create and produce the intro and outro music. Students use their phones to record the interviews and then they are sent for production and editing. In a distance learning environment, students conduct remote interviews using web conferencing or recorded phone calls.

Mr. Luukkonen edits and produces the interviews. He uses this time to assess the students according to predetermined success criteria. As this podcast continues, he hopes to have students participate in the production and editing. Once the podcasts are completed, they are uploaded to Anchor.fm and the SJT Immigration Project podcast can be found on all major podcast platforms

The impact of this assessment strategy on student learning is clear. "It is great to see kids learning about the people around them. Family members they interview are full of wisdom and interesting stories, and students get to learn about these sometimes 'hidden' family stories," the teacher said.

Scan this QR code to find the SJT Immigration Project podcast on Spotify.

As a class, students get to see that immigration stories are both uniquely individual, yet very similar in many ways. "They love working on this project because it is work that is non-traditional and offers them some choice," he says. "And it allows them to share with a much wider audience." Mr. Luukkonen's students say that it's a complicated assessment, but that they are engaged and interested due to the collective feeling that his class is sharing very important immigration stories.

Podcasts provide students with the opportunity to create, produce, and present their information to a wider audience (not just peers). Creating podcasts encourages students to use creative and critical thinking skills as they engage in interviewing others. There is potential for significant learning that occurs during the creation of podcasts not to mention the ability to determine what students have learned and what they still need to learn from listening to their submissions.

Written Summaries

Written summaries are another way for students to synthesize what they know. We could have included these in Playlist 3, on composing, but we placed them here because they are useful in building the knowledge of other students. These summaries can be used to assess understanding and to provide additional insights to others. As you may have noted from the tools in this playlist, the assessment opportunity is embedded in a task that allows others, such as peers, family members, or a broader audience to benefit from the knowledge and skills gained by the individual student.

There are two types of summaries used by student writers, and each has its unique purposes. The first is the *précis,* a brief summary of another text or experience (video, lab, etc.) that contains the main points but little embellishment. It is usually six to eight sentences in length, although a short reading may reduce the number of sentences to four. A second type is the *evaluation summary*. Like the précis, it is brief and focuses on the main points of the reading or experience. Unlike the précis, it concludes with a statement of the student writer's opinions and insights. All summaries possess three common characteristics:

> They are shorter than the original piece.
>
> They paraphrase the author's words.
>
> They focus on the main ideas only.

Twitter Notes. Ms. Adebayo's fourth-grade class has been working on using summaries as a means to check for understanding after a lesson, activity, or reading, for example. Although her students are unaware of Twitter, they are very competent in understanding a 280-character maximum. "Although my students are not on Twitter, I have them apply the same structure to their writing summary."

Her strategy, which she calls "Twitter Notes," challenges students to answer a prompt, summarize a story or reflect on their learning in 280 characters max (modeled after the maximum amount of characters allowed in a tweet).

"One of the highlights of using twitter notes in my class is watching the students critically think about what the most significant details are to include. My students spend quite a bit of time processing and vetting out unnecessary information to ensure their twitter notes are as clear and detailed as possible."

Students in Ms. Adebayo's class have the option of how to submit these summaries for assessment. Some use a Google Slides program wherein each summary is located on a new slide. As the year progresses, the students add more and more slides. (Figure 14 includes Ms. Adebayo's Google Slide template; it can also be accessed by

14 TWITTER NOTES TEMPLATE

Scan this QR code to find Ms. Adebayo's Google Slide template.

Student responses to the clarity questions exist across content areas. The videos below show students responding to the three clarity questions.

A student responds to the three clarity questions using a history lesson on the Gilded Age.

A student responds to the three clarity questions using a history lesson on industrialization, inequality, and immigration.

A student responds to the three clarity questions using a math lesson on random assignments in statistics.

resources.corwin.com/
AssessmentPlaybook

using the QR code.) Others track summaries using a documents program. Either way students are welcome to include links, pictures or anything else that can support their summary.

Twitter Notes can also serve older students as well, whether using a templated version like Ms. Adebayo or actually using the Twitter platform (the minimum age for this platform is thirteen and we suggest that you have parent permission to use the site). The idea of small 280-character summaries (sometimes called microblogging) forces our students to make deliberate decisions about what to include and exclude when constructing their passage. This strategy transcends disciplines, as this skill is vital regardless of the content students are learning. Should you decide to use the actual Twitter platform in the classroom, we suggest having an understanding of how the program works as well as an understanding of the potential risks of using Twitter. Developed with UNESCO, Twitter has created a "Teaching and Learning with Twitter" guide that can be found at https://about.twitter.com/content/dam/about-twitter/company/twitter-for-good/en/teaching-learning-with-twitter-unesco.pdf. We suggest taking time to look through the guide as Twitter can be a very powerful tool in the classroom, when used prudently.

Clarity Question Responses

We identified three questions useful in increasing the clarity of lessons:

➡ What am I learning today?

➡ Why am I learning this?

➡ How will I know that I have learned it? (Fisher et al., 2016, p. 27)

It turns out that these are useful questions to guide students' responses to the lessons as they allow teachers to determine what students learned, if they see relevance in the lessons, and if they recognize their own learning. In addition, when students respond to these three questions and they are shared with peers, there is an opportunity to solidify the lessons and maximize clarity and impact.

Amy Amato has students record their responses to these three clarity questions twice per week. Each day, some students are tasked with responding but no one does it every day. She has a schedule for her students so that they know when it is their turn. The students record on Flipgrid and submit for their teacher and peers to see.

As Ms. Amato says, "When I review these short videos, I get a sense of what parts of the lesson really resonated with students. I also get to hear if my attempts to make learning relevant hit the mark and if they know that they are learning. The start of the year was a bit bumpy and it seemed more like compliance. Now, students practice what they want to say so that they are ready. My students tell me that they really focus on the lessons more because they know that they will be sharing their thinking about these questions with the class."

istock/praetorianphoto

Students need opportunities to explain to others.

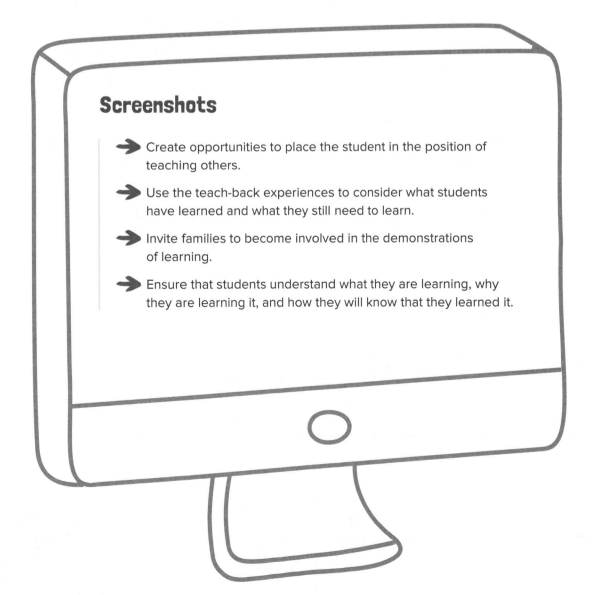

Screenshots

➡ Create opportunities to place the student in the position of teaching others.

➡ Use the teach-back experiences to consider what students have learned and what they still need to learn.

➡ Invite families to become involved in the demonstrations of learning.

➡ Ensure that students understand what they are learning, why they are learning it, and how they will know that they learned it.

PLAYLIST 3: ASSESSMENT THROUGH COMPOSING

Sabrina Burnette's sixth-grade English students are poised to begin their weekly timed-writing assessment. Every Tuesday during synchronous learning, students write for fifteen minutes on a topic related to their unit of study. Although this is a distance learning class, the practice is a carryover from her physical classroom. The target book the students are reading is *Look Both Ways: A Tale Told in Ten Blocks* (Reynolds, 2019), a choice book her students selected as part of their unit on Empathy and Community. "I've set up a Google Doc for each one of you and the prompt is on it. Keep in mind that this is timed writing, so you've got 15 minutes," said the teacher. Using the live widgets feature in Google Classroom, Ms. Burnette is able to see the work of her students in real time. This week's prompt is about the use of repetition of images and words as a literary device, and the students have been asked to discuss two examples of their choice. "These weekly timed-writing exercises are low-stakes assessments that give me a window on their composition processes as well as their comprehension of the material," she said. "I analyze these short writing pieces to figure out what needs to happen next."

Ms. Burnette uses these timed-writing events to differentiate instruction. She has recorded general writing videos of three to five minutes focused on a specific aspect of composition, from punctuation, to grammar, organization, voice, word choice, sentence composition, and organization. From this library, she selects ones that will be useful for those students making the same errors consistently. "Students watch these during asynchronous learning, and I've built a few questions into them just to check on their understanding of the content of the video," she explained. "Not everyone gets a video," she continued, "but I can send a video on noun–verb agreement to three students, and a different one on word choice to two others. These interactive videos allow me to provide instruction based on need and I can check in with them during synchronous sessions to see if they are able to apply the learning. It's actually brought more precision to my teaching."

Composition as Assessment

Writing is arguably the assessment type that lends itself best to measures of student progress. Because it is used across the spectrum—assessment *for* learning, *as* learning, and *of* learning—we will restrict our focus to the first. Having said that, you will see other uses for composition appear in other playlists. The permanent product nature of written work makes it easy for teachers to thoughtfully analyze and assess what students know and don't know.

We want to further distinguish *composition* as an umbrella term for all the sophisticated skills that go into the act of writing. While *writing* itself is a general term for the action of putting ideas onto paper or in a digital format, composition includes all of those cognitive skills and processes that are needed to do so. Composition requires planning, knowledge, mechanics, conventions, and voice. Writers must consider the audience and purpose, as well as the structure to be used. The three major composition structures are narrative, informational, and argumentation, and these are tied to purposes for writing:

➡ Narrative structures are used to convey real or imaginary experiences.

➡ Informational structures are used to explain and inform.

➡ Argumentation structures are used to persuade using emotion, logic, and reasoning.

Composition traverses all the subject areas and its structures vary somewhat depending on the purposes. If you're a science teacher, much of the composition your students do comes in the form of lab reports and making claims with supporting evidence, which are argumentation. If you're a math educator, you probably ask your students to explain the mathematical thinking they used to solve a problem, which is also a form of argumentation. If you are an elementary educator, you probably ask your students to write opinion letters to the principal, which is a third form of argumentation. In other words, the broader compositional purpose encompasses many genres of writing (a lab report, a math reflection, a persuasive letter). Regardless of your content area or the age of your students, there is some element of composition occurring in your distance learning classroom.

Rubrics as an Assessment Tool

Rubrics are widely used as a way to both teach and assess writing. These "illustrative scoring mechanisms" provide writers with guidance in the form of criteria and further describe a range of work quality (Ghaffar, Khairallah, & Salloum, 2020, p. 1). There are two types of rubric formats we'll discuss in this playlist: *holistic* and *analytic*. A third type, called a *single-point* rubric, is suited for self-assessment, which we will discuss in Playlist 4. Holistic rubrics are primarily used to assess a writing product and are particularly common for large-scale writing assessments. An advantage of holistic rubrics, such as the one in Figure 15, is that they are easily understood by students (at least the score) because they are broad. However, a disadvantage is that are less useful for giving specific feedback and both the student and the teacher may struggle with scoring papers that fall between categories.

Analytic rubrics resolve some of the concerns about holistic rubrics by separating the expectations into their own categories. They are useful for defining specific points for the writer to focus on in subsequent drafts. The analytic rubric in Figure 16 is especially useful in assessment for learning, as both the student and the teacher can focus on specific elements for improvement. One caution with analytic rubrics is that they can quickly contain more words and technical terminology than younger students are able to handle. In fact, take another look at any of your favorite analytic rubrics. Many are written for teachers, not for students. For this reason, consider co-constructing rubrics with students to encourage active participation and to ensure that developmentally appropriate language is used. Middle school students in a study of co-constructed writing rubrics demonstrated improved dispositions to writing and increased writing skills (Ghaffar et al., 2020).

CONSIDER CO-CONSTRUCTING RUBRICS WITH STUDENTS TO ENCOURAGE ACTIVE PARTICIPATION AND TO ENSURE THAT DEVELOPMENTALLY APPROPRIATE LANGUAGE IS USED.

15 **HOLISTIC RUBRIC**

Levels of Success	Descriptors
3 **Exceeds Expectations**	The writing is organized, accurate, and easy to read. The prompt is fully answered. There are few errors of mechanics or conventions and these do not interfere with the meaning.
2 **Meets Expectations**	The writing is mostly organized and accurate. The prompt is mostly answered. There are some errors of mechanics or conventions, but these mostly do not interfere with the meaning.
1 **Still Working and Progressing**	The writing is disorganized and hard to understand. The prompt is not addressed and the writing is off topic. There are many errors of mechanics or conventions and they interfere with the meaning.

16 **ANALYTIC RUBRIC**

Criteria	1–Still Working	2–Meets Expectations	3–Exceeds Expectations
Organization	Organization is confusing and is hard for the reader to follow.	Organization is logical and the reader is mostly able to follow.	Organization is logical and easy to follow for the reader.
Sources of Information	The information is not accurate or draws from unreliable sources.	The information is accurate and credible.	The information is accurate and credible and includes sources not shared in class.
Addresses the Prompt	The prompt is not addressed and instead is off topic.	Some information required by the prompt is missing.	The information fully addresses the prompt.
Mechanics and Conventions	There are numerous mechanics and convention errors (e.g., punctuation, capitalization, spelling, grammar) that interfere with the reader's understanding.	The few mechanics and convention errors (e.g., punctuation, capitalization, spelling, grammar) do not interfere with the reader's understanding.	The mechanics and conventions are largely accurate (e.g., punctuation, capitalization, spelling, grammar).

Co-Constructing Rubrics

Third-grade teacher Jana Lieberman co-constructed a writing rubric with her students early in the school year. "I've done this before in my face-to-face classroom using chocolate chip cookies," she said. "In distance learning, I can't distribute those, so instead I asked them to bring their favorite toy to our next synchronous session." After each child introduced their favorite toy and explained what they liked about it, Ms. Lieberman began the discussion about the qualities of good toys. She took notes on the virtual whiteboard as students talked about the need to be able to do lots of things with it, that it wouldn't easily break, and of course the fun factor. After she listed them, the teacher said, "Those ideas you came up with are called *criteria*. Criteria are kind of like the qualities that you look for in a good toy." She then moved the discussion to writing criteria. "How do we know something is good writing? What qualities should we look for?" Her students initially talked about the fact that the words should be spelled correctly and the handwriting should be neat. With her help, she began to introduce new ideas, such as focus, style, and ideas. She then gave them a template to use in their breakout rooms, with the criteria they had agreed upon written on the left side, but with the individual cells still blank. "When they came back together, each group shared what they had completed," she said. "There was no expectation that they would fill all the cells. But it gave me a springboard to finalize a rubric that contained their ideas and language," she said.

You don't need to feel compelled to co-construct every rubric with every class. It isn't practical for secondary teachers who teach multiple sections to be able to use a custom rubric for each period. However, soliciting some feedback in advance of the rubric development can be useful for building a shared understanding of expectations, as well as a sense of ownership.

Interactive Notebooks

Capturing student writing for assessment purposes, especially the kind of low-stakes short writing that we discuss in this playlist, can be something of a challenge. You probably relied on notebooks in your face-to-face classroom. In distance learning (or even in hybrid learning), you may want to consider using digital interactive notebooks for students in Grades 3 and above. A benefit of using interactive digital notebooks is that you can find their work without having your students go through separate submissions.

Interactive digital notebooks can be Google Slides that look a lot like a physical notebook. Use a template (these are widely available) that includes tabs that portion off different "pages" so you and your students can easily find particular elements.

These links should correspond with your organizational structure for your class. For example, you may want to set up tabs and label them according to the concepts you're teaching in a unit (e.g., Westward Expansion or Properties of Matter) or by activity (e.g., Exit Tickets, Vocabulary). Some teachers have students use a new interactive notebook for each unit of instruction. In addition to their writing, you can add activities, materials, and other handouts to their notebook, so they always have what they need. Set up your interactive notebook as a master so that you can update as needed. You can then update the students' notebooks through a Share link your students have. (See Figure 17 for an example from a biology class).

17 INTERACTIVE NOTEBOOK PAGE

1.6 Characteristics of Life

← BACK **to divider**

Instructions: Watch and answer the questions in the PlayPosit.

Characteristic	Definition	Example
Made of 1 or More Cells		
Displays Organization		
Grows and Develops		
Reproduces		
Responds to Stimuli		
Requires Energy		
Maintains Homeostasis		
Adaptations Evolve Over Time		

Generative Sentences

Student composition is of great value; getting them started can be a challenge. After all, if they don't produce anything, you don't have anything to assess. Generative sentences can be of great value in spurring on writing. It is an extension of the given word approach described by Fearn and Farnan (2001). We have used this as a springboard to propel student writing forward by scaffolding their writing from the word, to the sentence, to the paragraph level.

It begins with a series of vocabulary words spotlighted in a unit. However, rather than asking students to write sentences containing each of the words, students are constrained by word conditions that require them to consider not only the semantics, but also the syntax and grammar required. We'll give you a chance to try one on your own:

Write a sentence where the word *atom* is in the third position in a sentence that is at least seven words long.

Did you do it? It took you a minute, right? And you had to make a bunch of decisions to do so. You had to think about the meaning of the word, but then you probably also had to decide what kind of atom. As the third word in the sentence, you probably said something like *"A hydrogen atom . . ."* Next, you had to build this out further into a longer sentence that fit the length: *"A hydrogen atom is made of one positive proton."* Hmm . . . that's correct, but it's kind of incomplete as a description. *"A hydrogen atom is made of one positive proton and one negative electron."* In doing so, you made decisions as a writer and as a science-literate person.

Now imagine that a middle school science teacher asks his students to do a series of these, like Marco Aguilera does with his students during his synchronous sessions. Once a week, they review current content vocabulary through writing. Mr. Aguilera has students compose five generative sentences using target vocabulary (see Figure 18).

"During your asynchronous time today, I want you to choose one of the sentences you wrote and use that in a paragraph that summarizes the science concept you've selected. Make sure that paragraph is a least five sentences long and add it to your science interactive notebook by the end of the day," said the teacher. He later commented, "I need to see how much they know, and writing is a great way to find out. Using generative sentences as a weekly routine lets them get started on something that they can finish independently."

18 GENERATIVE SENTENCES

Word	Placement	Length
atom	3rd	> 7 words
bond	4th	< 8 words
ions	1st	= 6 words
mass	2nd	≥ 7 words
nucleus	last	between 8–10 words

Practice writing your own generative sentence assignments based on your own content.

 Available for download at **resources.corwin.com/AssessmentPlaybook**

Power Writing to Assess Fluency

Composing requires two different kinds of fluency: the conceptual fluency of thought, and scribing fluency to put those ideas down on paper or screen. Composing, therefore, is in part the ability to push ideas from brain to pencil or keyboard. We have long used Power Writing as a way to gauge the writing fluency progress of our students, particularly in being able to generate a volume of writing.

Power writing consists of short daily timed writing events designed to build writing fluency (Fearn & Farnan, 2001). The premise is simple: three one-minute rounds of daily writing, either on paper or in their interactive notebooks, with the direction to "write as much as you can, as well as you can." At the end of each round, students count the number of words they have written and record the amount. They reread what they have written and circle any errors they noticed whether mechanics or syntax. We don't ask them to correct them; circling the error lets us know they noticed the error and it is not necessary to reteach them the skill.

What we have noticed time and again is that the number of words written increases between the first and third rounds. Students record their daily "personal best" on digital graph paper so they can see their own progress. We have used this same technique with second graders and high school seniors. In some cases, we provide a word or phrase to inspire them, but they aren't required to actually use it in their Power

Writing. Primary teachers adjust their Power Writing to mimic what Clay (2013) calls writing vocabulary by asking students to write all the words they know on their whiteboard.

Using Google Forms for Paragraph Response

Students are often asked to write short constructed responses to assessment items that include a prompt and source information. The writing prompt itself serves as a priming function, and if properly understood the writer will move forward in the correct direction. However, students may rush past the details of the prompt and misunderstand the relationship between the prompt and the source information and thus write a paragraph that is off topic or incomplete. Understanding the prompt and accompanying information is key. However, assessing their understanding of the prompt itself is less common. Teach students about parsing writing prompts and assess their understanding of them using a digital form (whether Google or Microsoft) to gain more insight into student thought processes. The process we have used is to engage the student in a series of inquiry questions prior to the writing task itself.

TEACH STUDENTS ABOUT PARSING WRITING PROMPTS AND ASSESS THEIR UNDERSTANDING OF THEM.

Source or Prompt
Key Question to drive paragraph response
Inquiry Planning Questions 1. Are there words in the source, prompt, or key question you do not understand or find confusing? 2. Does the source or prompt have a biased perspective or multiple perspectives? 3. What does the source say in your own words?
Please provide a paragraph response to the key question:

Scan this QR code for an example of what this looks like in Google Forms.

online resources   Available for download at **resources.corwin.com/AssessmentPlaybook**

Allowing students to use a "forms" structure to answer in a paragraph response has benefits for teachers working remotely from their classroom. First, the forms program consolidates all answers. This becomes especially important for the first inquiry planning question: *Are there words in the source, prompt, or key question you do not understand or find confusing?*

A quick glance at the summary document after all students complete the form can provide immediate feedback about terms or vocabulary that might be confusing. Middle school humanities teacher Julie Nguyen recognized the power and efficiency of this model when she prompted her students to write about immigration. She notes, "As I was reviewing their answers about confusing words, I noticed about 15 students indicated they were confused about the terms *refugees* and *immigrants*." While this may seem alarming, it is what Ms. Nguyen did with that information that was striking. "I knew my students could not properly complete this assignment without knowing the difference between those terms, so instead of collecting this assignment, I dedicated the next lesson to clarifying what the students found confusing." This information was gleaned from the form in less than one minute and completely altered Ms. Nguyen's instruction.

The One-Pager

Much like a Twitter Notes Summary from Playlist 2, the one-pager provides a medium for students to summarize their thoughts and key takeaways from aspects of our instruction. Unlike a traditional summary, the one-pager includes both text and images. For a one-pager to be successful, students take what they've learned and include their highlights on a single page. The application of the one-pager assignment is seemingly limitless. Although originally intended to use to summarize novels, these can extend to lesson summaries, summaries about a TED Talk, current events, podcast, film, a laboratory, or simply a summary of a unit of study (among even more applications). For one-pagers to yield a higher impact, there are certain steps that should be considered (see Figure 19). The mixed media approach to creating one-pagers can encourage students to leverage multiple dispositions as they complete this assessment. By allowing students to have aspects of voice and choice in their completion of these assignments, we can foster their ability to critically engage with the content using skills that are familiar to them.

19 CONSIDERATIONS FOR SUCCESSFUL ONE-PAGERS

1. Choose elements you want students to put onto their one-pagers: for example, quotations, key themes, literary elements, discussion of style, important characters or dates, connections to other disciplines, connections to their lives, connections to modern culture.

2. Create a layout using the shapes tool in PowerPoint or something similar.

3. Connect your instructions to your layout. Make it clear which elements should go in which area of your template (this is especially important in younger grades).

4. Rubrics created for these assignments should draw directly from success criteria and should be discussed prior to giving this assessment.

5. Digital one-pagers can be created using a variety of programs (depending on the level of comfort students and teachers have), but are just as effective if built in a word processing program.

6. One-pagers should be displayed for all students to participate in a Virtual Gallery walk. This is especially true if the one-pager is being used for a larger summary (unit, film, etc.).

Source: Adapted from Potash (2019). https://www.cultofpedagogy.com/one-pagers

Annotations as Assessment

Annotation is a form of student notetaking where students mark passages with questions, connections to information, and other comments. This practice is widely used with texts in every subject and the advancement of digital annotation technology makes it possible for students to do so in electronic textbooks, readings, and videos. Of course, students can also annotate on paper texts using pen or pencil. We like to teach students three foundational annotations:

1. Underlining key ideas so that they learn the difference between supporting details and important messages

2. Circling words and phrases that are confusing so that they learn to monitor their own understanding

3. Creating marginal notes in which they restate information or ideas in their own words so that they learn to synthesize and summarize

Students may choose to use other annotations, but these three seem to us to be valuable in developing students' habits (Fisher, Frey, & Law, 2020).

Fifth-grade teacher Jenny Harjo requires her students to annotate complex readings across the day. "It helps them to dig down more deeply into the text to understand its meaning," she said. On occasion she collects their annotations to determine how each child is progressing in terms of reading comprehension. Ms. Harjo alternates between digital and paper for texts and annotations, depending on what's available. During their social studies unit on early settlements in North America, they read about the treatment of indigenous peoples as Europeans immigrated to the continent. She provided the text digitally to her students and they used it during a synchronous close reading lesson, annotating either on a printed copy or digitally. "I gave them the choice of their preferred mode, and I collected their annotated copies to learn about their responses to the text and the lesson," said Ms. Harjo.

There are three items Ms. Harjo looks for in her students' annotations. The first is how often a student made a connection, posed a question, or identified a key concept. The second quality she looks for is related to the targeted skill or concept being taught in the lesson. In this case, she wanted students to critically analyze the text to identify what information was missing. "During the lesson we discussed the use of coded language that obscured what might have really occurred," said the teacher. "For instance, we spent time with a sentence that said that the people of the region 'relocated' but it never said under what circumstances. So, I'm looking for evidence of that discussion." The third element she looks for is evidence that annotation occurred beyond the first reading. "There's a deepening of learning that should happen throughout the close reading. I want to see if they're continuing to annotate as the repeated readings and discussions go on so I have them change the color of their highlighter." Ms. Harjo's checklist is in Figure 20. "I don't want this assessment to be too time consuming for me, but I do want to get a sense of what they are learning or not learning. Taking a look at their annotations gives me a heads-up about who I might need to meet with for some follow-up small group instruction."

20 ANNOTATIONS CHECKLIST

☐ **Quality of annotations:** There are connections to other ideas inside and outside the text, questions, and notations of key concepts in the reading.

☐ **Target skill or concept:** The focus of the lesson's learning intention is evidenced in the annotations.

☐ **Depth of annotations:** The annotations build across the lesson and represent increasing understanding.

Five-Word Summary

Many students have difficulty in being able to summarize a text without either retelling the whole thing or being too brief and in doing so omitting important information. Five-word summaries, much like generative sentences, assist students in beginning a summary during synchronous instruction in order to complete it independently during asynchronous time. An added benefit is that it promotes oral language use and peer collaboration.

1. Students read a piece of text and independently choose five words that represent the reading.

2. They talk with a partner to reach consensus on a new list of five words that they have co-constructed.

3. They join another partnership, now with four students, and reach agreements on a final five-word list that represents the text.

4. Each then creates their own written summary of the text, using the five words agreed upon by the group.

These five-word summaries also highlight the "big ideas" often subsumed in so much detail, and thus can provide the "coat hanger" that students can hang ideas on.

High school biology teacher Ben Rivera uses five-word summaries of technical texts for students to write in their digital interactive notebooks. "It's really important that they get the details down in their notes without just copying what they've read. They need to synthesize," said Mr. Rivera. After reading a passage on diseases of the coronary system in their A&P manual, Mr. Rivera gives each student a few minutes to independently list five words from the reading that they believe are significant.

After the students have completed this first stage, he moves them into breakout rooms of two students. "Remember, you and your partner need to come up with a shared list of five words," he says. He moves in and out of several breakout rooms to observe their negotiations and to listen for correct language use. After five minutes, he collapses the rooms by half, so that each breakout room now consists of two pairs, a total of four students. "I go into the participants box and pair up room 1 and 2, 3 and 4, and so on," he explained. Each pair is equipped with their shared list, and now the goal is for the four students to finalize a single list of five words. The whole process takes about twenty minutes in total from start to finish.

Students return to the virtual main room for final instructions. "You've now got five words that you and the other people in your group finalized. During your asynchronous time, write your own summary in your interactive notebooks. I'll be checking those tomorrow for accuracy so that you've got accurate notes about arteriosclerosis and atherosclerosis."

Composing is an important tool in your assessment toolkit. Students write in every subject (not just English or reading) as they synthesize, summarize, and apply what they are learning. Perhaps there has been some reluctance to utilize writing in distance learning because the platforms can be intimidating. Keep in mind that students can also write on paper and on whiteboards, as well as utilizing digital formats. What's key is to have some go-to methods for assessing their writing in order to make instruction decisions about what happens next in teaching.

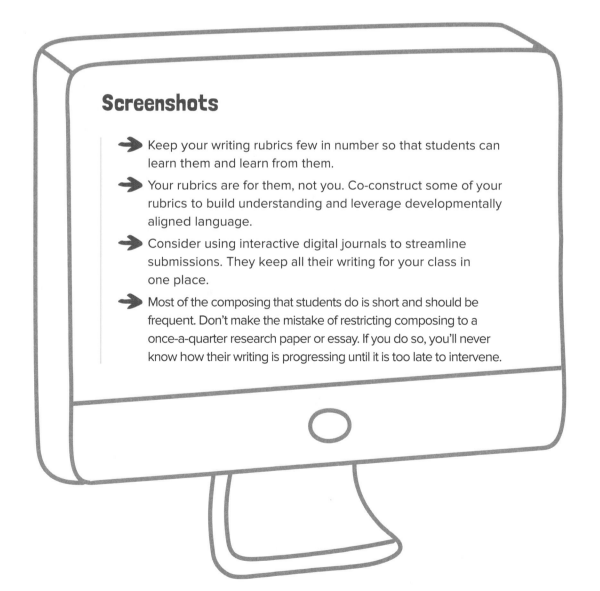

Screenshots

➜ Keep your writing rubrics few in number so that students can learn them and learn from them.

➜ Your rubrics are for them, not you. Co-construct some of your rubrics to build understanding and leverage developmentally aligned language.

➜ Consider using interactive digital journals to streamline submissions. They keep all their writing for your class in one place.

➜ Most of the composing that students do is short and should be frequent. Don't make the mistake of restricting composing to a once-a-quarter research paper or essay. If you do so, you'll never know how their writing is progressing until it is too late to intervene.

PLAYLIST 4: SELF- AND PEER ASSESSMENT

Grade 8-science student Raya McNamara's finger is hovering over the "submit" button. Her teacher has sent an exit ticket as a Google Form that asks for a constructed response about the morning's virtual session: "People often say that the way they see is with their eyes. But there's more to sight than just the eyes. Think about today's lesson. How would you explain the missing information?" Raya wrote, "It's the brain that actually sees because it interprets what the eyes capture. The optic nerve carries the signal." The second question on the exit ticket is about her confidence in her answer. "How confident do you feel about today's lesson/skill? Would you be successful if today's content was on a test?"

Raya had chosen 4 but now reconsiders. She realizes that she has a new confusion. Raya remembers that the teacher talked about how the image is upside down to the eyes, but flips so that a person understands it. But how does that happen? Now she's not so sure. She changes to a 3 and submits the form. Sometimes the teacher asks the students why they chose the confidence level, as this helps students like Raya show where she has doubts and this can provide evidence for the teacher and Raya to explore these doubts more fully.

Raya's teacher, Jalen Michaels, will receive exit tickets like Raya's over the next several hours as his students work asynchronously on their classes. For Mr. Michaels, it is a way for him to teach responsively through feedback received using this simple assessment process. But for Raya, it accomplishes even more. Through self-assessment, she is able to reflect on what she knows and notice what she doesn't know. These are crucial components of the self-monitoring process. By asking Raya to report her confidence, not just her content knowledge, she is developing her ability to calibrate her predictions to her performance.

The Power of Self-Assessment

The relationship between motivation and achievement is a strong one. Students who achieve at high levels not only possess cognitive knowledge, but also are able to engage in self-appraisal, which is one's own judgment about the quality of the work they have completed (Spinath, Spinath, Harlaar, & Plomin, 2006). Just as important, when students regardless of their cognitive knowledge receive feedback from assessments it can be motivating to appreciate where they have advanced and this too can spur them to learn more—of course provided it is feedback that includes information about "where to go next" for the student to learn, and is done in a timely and positive manner. The ability to self-appraise is acquired through lots of chances to do so. Importantly, quality self-assessments require students to use their metacognitive skills and move beyond yes/no dichotomous answers. We offer this as a contrast to some of the universal responses discussed in an earlier playlist, which provide feedback to the teacher but may not necessarily stretch a student's thinking.

Self-appraisal is at the heart of Visible Learning. These students "exhibit the self-regulatory attributes that seem most desirable for learners (self-monitoring, self-evaluation, self-assessment, self-teaching)" (Hattie, 2009, p. 22). These are fueled by a constellation of metacognitive skills that allow a learner to

> **THE ABILITY TO SELF-APPRAISE IS ACQUIRED THROUGH LOTS OF CHANCES TO DO SO.**

- ➡ Plan for the task
- ➡ Monitor one's learning
- ➡ Review and revise corrected work

Metacognition (thinking about one's thinking) isn't solely about knowing when you know something (Flavell, 1985). It is also, as in the case of Raya, the ability to recognize when you don't know something. The ability to think metacognitively helps a student make decisions about their own learning. Learners who are metacognitively aware are accurately able to articulate their own strengths and plan for the use of other strategies, including help-seeking, that will help them get "unstuck." As John likes to say, "It's knowing what to do when you don't know what to do." Think of self-assessments as feedback to self about whether one is on the right track or not.

The Power of Peer Assessments

Peer assessments enhance the feedback loop. The student receiving the feedback profits from another set of eyes, to be sure, but arguably the larger benefit is to the one posing the feedback. Each time a student provides a peer assessment, they deepen their own understanding of the content and quality. Little wonder that the evidence on peer tutoring is pretty convincing. With an effect size of 0.51, peer tutoring has been widely studied for its effects on both the tutor and the tutee (Hattie, n.d.). In many cases, the benefit is even stronger for the former compared to the latter. The opportunity to think about someone else's learning, not just your own, is invaluable.

The other major advantage is that it teaches students to learn how to "error detect," how to understand how there can be other ways to resolve and solve problems, how to give feedback, and learn the critical skills of critique (the ideas not the person). These are powerful lessons for students to learn how then to self-assess and become their own teachers.

In terms of the relative accuracy of peer assessments, they are comparable to teacher assessments, if properly taught and implemented (Sanchez, Atkinson, Koenka, Moshontz, & Cooper, 2017). Those moderating factors of peer assessment include the following:

→ Setting a climate for learning that is nonthreatening

→ Using rubrics to support the process

→ Providing teacher modeling and ample practice opportunities

THE STUDENT RECEIVING THE FEEDBACK PROFITS FROM ANOTHER SET OF EYES, BUT ARGUABLY THE LARGER BENEFIT IS TO THE ONE POSING THE FEEDBACK.

As one example, middle school students were taught and then utilized online peer assessments as part of a performing arts course. The students who used the peer assessments reported higher levels of satisfaction, self-efficacy, and motivation compared to control classes where peer assessment was not used (Hsia, Huang, & Hwang, 2016). Taken together, the effectiveness of self-assessments and peer assessments amplify student learning. Further, they provide an added dimension to your assessment map beyond reliance solely on teacher assessments. We will discuss examples of each.

Know/Show Charts

Middle school geography teacher Curtis Brown is taking his class on a tour of landforms in Central America. Not physically, of course, but using video shot using a drone. There are three he is focusing on in today's asynchronous lesson, to be completed before the live virtual session.

"My learning intention today is for them to be able to identify the Pacific coastal plain, the Caribbean lowlands, and the mountainous core that forms the central part of this land mass," he explained. "By the end of the week, they will have examined those in Mexico and South America as well." His success criteria for the week are posted on his learning management system and he revisits them during each live session.

At the end of the week, students write or complete a Google Form version of a Know/Show chart (Figure 21). They list what they have learned in the Know column and propose a way they can Show their learning. Mr. Brown reviews each student's submission and selects one item in the "Show" column for students to complete. For Adam, a student in his class, Mr. Brown selected "make a virtual poster of images of landmasses in South America" from the list the boy had proposed. For Selena, another student in the class, the teacher chose "make a compare/contrast chart of similarities and differences of climates in five regions of Mexico" from her proposed list.

"I get a really good idea of what they know when I see what they propose to demonstrate it," Mr. Brown said. "None of the proposed tasks are large ones, and they often propose things like a short Flipgrid video to explain their thinking. Because they know I am going to choose one from their lists, they really have to give some thought about what they're able to do."

21 **KNOW/SHOW CHART**

What do you know about the locations, landforms, and climates of Mexico, Central America, and South America?	How can you show what you know?
1.	
2.	
3.	
4.	
5.	

Source: Fisher, D., Frey, N., & Gonzalez Ojeda, A. (2020). *On-your-feet guide: Distance learning by design, grades 3–12*. Thousand Oaks, CA: Corwin.

Single-Point Rubrics for Self-Assessment

The strategies in this playlist focus on students being able to assess their own learning. To do so, they require tools. Specifically, tools that they understand and can use. These tools allow them to monitor their own learning, make adjustments to their learning, and increase the likelihood that students will seek out, and accept, the feedback that you provide.

As you probably noticed, the Know/Show chart was a powerful way for students to identify what they learned and the various ways that they could show it. Single point rubrics also allow students to identify what they know and can do compared with the criteria for success. In Playlist 3, on composing, we shared a number of rubrics that were analytic or holistic. More traditionally, those are used by the teacher to assess student learning, recognizing that they are really only useful if students know what is in the rubric in advance of completing tasks.

The single-point rubric is different. Essentially, you take the success criteria, or the level that is proficient on an analytic rubric and use that as the criterion against which students assess their understanding. As with all rubrics, they can be co-constructed with students or developed by the teacher. When developed by the teacher, it's important to ensure that students understand the items on the rubric.

Typically, a single-point rubric has the criteria and descriptors in the middle column of three, with left column being reserved for areas of need and the right for areas that indicate performance or understanding meeting or exceeding the expectations. The first graders in Lana Thibodeaux's class were learning to construct simple maps. They had already created maps of their homes and were working on mapping their local community. Ms. Thibodeaux taught them the cardinal directions and they practiced online responding to questions such as "Is the house north or south of the park?"

Ms. Thibodeaux shared a sample map with her students and then discussed the criteria for success that was included in the single-point rubric (see Figure 22). She used picture symbols as reminders for students so that they could use the tool on their own. She also included words to aid family members in talking with their children about the maps.

Carmi used this single-point rubric to review his work. He made a mark in the happy face column for directions, building, and streets. And he made a mark in the needs work column for map symbols. When asked about it, he said, "I have five buildings, so that is

22 SINGLE-POINT RUBRIC ON CREATE A MAP

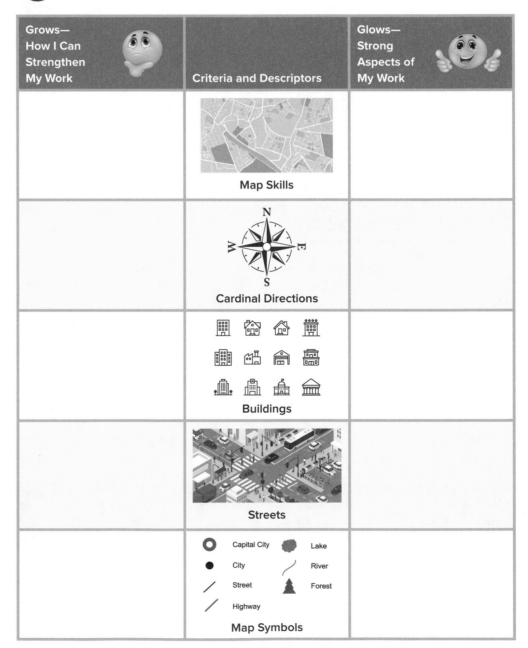

Grows— How I Can Strengthen My Work	Criteria and Descriptors	Glows— Strong Aspects of My Work
	Map Skills	
	Cardinal Directions	
	Buildings	
	Streets	
	Map Symbols	

Image sources: Grows, Glows: iStock.com/Tigatelu; Map Skills: iStock.com/reklamlar; Cardinal Directions: iStock.com/Lubo Ivanko; Buildings: iStock.com/rambo182; Streets: iStock.com/elenabs

good. I have the N and stuff so that is good. And look at my streets! I have four streets. I only have two of these, pointing to the symbols. Can you help?"

Single-point rubrics are not limited to use in elementary school. High school science teacher Tracy Glass wanted her students to propose a researchable question and engage in an investigation. They had significant choice in the topic, provided that they could make a connection with the contents of the class. Students would write their paper and present their findings to the class in small groups during breakout sessions. The single-point rubric she used for students to self-assess their work can be found in Figure 23.

23 SINGLE-POINT RUBRIC FOR SCIENCE INVESTIGATION

Grows—How I Can Strengthen My Work	Criteria and Descriptors *for learning about decomposing and composing numbers into groups of hundreds, tens and ones*	Glows—Strong Aspects of My Work
	Identify a topic that aligns with course content (make sure you have approval before starting the project).	
	Develop a thesis statement or claim that you can investigate.	
	Collect and organize evidence that **supports** your thesis or claim.	
	Collect and organize evidence that **refutes** your thesis or claim.	
	Create an outline for your paper that includes your thesis or claim as well as your major talking points (make sure we talk before you start writing).	

Anayeli noted that she was strong in all of the areas except that all of her evidence supported her claim. As she said, "I have tons of research about flossing. I know, it's a strange topic. But I wanted to know more about why people say we should floss. But I don't have anything that says we should not floss. So, I need to go back and see if I am missing something. It wouldn't be on the rubric if I can't do it, so there must be something out there."

Note that the rubric did not specifically relate to flossing or any other topic. But it did cause the student to think about her response and what she still needed to do. She ended up finding studies suggesting that flossing was not that important that she had not found before because, as she says, she was searching for "the benefits of flossing."

Single-Point Rubrics for Peer Assessment

Single-point rubrics can also be combined with peer feedback. This can serve as a valuable assessment of student learning as well as an opportunity to continue learning. Peer evaluation through single-point rubrics can look like this in a distance learning environment:

→ Teacher and students can engage in the process of co-construction of success criteria.

→ Success criteria is then utilized in a single-point rubric.

→ Upon draft completion of the assignment or project, students submit their assignment to the teacher who will track the assignments and remove names for anonymity.

→ Students are placed in small groups (using web conferencing programs) and are given a collection of completed assignments, along with the single-point rubric. We find that using a program such as Google Docs works well for student collaboration.

→ Single-point rubrics are completed collaboratively by the small groups of students and students can use this feedback as they work toward the final drafts (remember the assignments they are providing assessments for are anonymous).

Applying the strategy in distance learning requires some explicit teaching about protocols and procedures. First, students must understand the indicators of each criterion on the rubric. And they need to understand that the conversation is intended for growth and learning. You may want to assign roles such as timekeeper, discussion director, and mood monitor, so that the process operates smoothly.

For example, the students in Peter Corrales's art class used a single-point rubric to provide feedback to one another. As Mr. Corrales noted, "There are technical aspects that we can focus on but remember, art is very personal. Just because you don't like something, or really like something, does not mean that it's better or worse. We've talked a lot about aesthetics and how beauty is in the eye of the beholder. At this point, we have sketches of our planned watercolors. They're just drafts and are meant to be improved. I've loaded the photos of the sketches into the docs so that you can see them and make comments, constructive ones, using the rubric. We're only using the first three topics because we haven't got to color yet. When we have some of the watercolors done, we'll focus on that part of the rubric as well." See Figure 24 for the rubric Mr. Corrales used.

As students evaluate and assess according to the single-point rubric, we would like to draw your attention to the categories of *areas that need work* and *evidence of exceeding standards*. The title of these categories can change according to the circumstances of your classroom; however, for this example we chose these two categories with the intention that students will highlight and find elements in the assignment that exceed or need work. The purpose of doing this is to ensure that students provide feedback and assessment of the actual product against well-defined success criteria.

24 SINGLE-POINT RUBRIC FOR ART

Areas That Need Work	Criteria and Descriptors	Evidence of Exceeding Standards
	Line How does the line lead your eye? Vertically? Horizontally? Is the line diagonal, straight or curved, thick or thin? *Is the use of line effective?*	
	Shape Consider the height and width of the items in the sketch. Are they in concert with each other? What shapes are used? *Are shapes used effectively?*	
	Space How does the artist use the area? What role does negative space play? What is in the positive space? *Is space used effectively?*	
	Color Consider the hue, value, and intensity. Are they in balance? Is the intentional use of warm or cool colors obvious? *Is color used effectively?*	

This is exactly what happened when Jacob said to Maricruz, "In your sketch of the bay, your eye goes right to the water. The line is super powerful. I can almost see the color that you'll have there. I think it will be deep blue so that it's different from the big grey ship that you have out in the water."

"Your use of space is also majorly impressive," Amal added. "Like the water is huge and the ship is small, like the feeling of being lonely or lost or something. It's really good. I want to see it when you're done. I hope we're in the same group for the next review."

Maricruz asked, "So, what can I do better?"

Amal responded. "I think, well, it's just a draft, but the shape of the ship is a little off. It looks too heavy on the top, you know? But that's not a big deal. Like in the real one it would be in proportion."

"Thanks for noticing that," Maricruz said. "I'm gonna make sure that I sketch that out a little better before I paint so that I get it right and people don't have to look at it twice, thinking that it's gonna fall over."

Color-Coded Feedback

The use of color-coded feedback can structure the peer interactions and improve learning. In its simplest form, color-coded feedback can provide specific information to students about the process of their learning. The color-coded aspect of assessment allows peers to evaluate each other and engage in metacognitive conversations. Here is an example of how color-coded feedback can work:

➡ Once students have completed a draft of their work, they exchange with their peer.

➡ Peer student evaluates/assesses student work according to established success criteria. Instead of giving feedback (written or oral) they simply highlight specific areas of the assignment with two different colors. One color to indicate "meeting success criteria" the other to indicate "approaching success criteria."

➡ Students return work to original owner, and each student must reflect on their process and determine why their peer indicated specific colors in specific areas on their assignment. That does not mean that they must agree with their peer, but rather think about why their peer coded their paper the way that they did.

➡ After reflection, the peers return together and have a conversation about the color-coded feedback and the process of their learning.

Utilizing web-conference programs, teachers can provide spaces for students to engage in video conversations about the feedback they provided each other. Depending on the size and complexity of the assignment, teachers should limit the number of feedback points and always ensure students are providing more positive feedback than negative (e.g., students must provide between 3 to 5 success points and 2 to 4 approaching points).

PEER ASSESSMENTS WORK BEST WHEN STUDENTS ARE TAUGHT HOW TO USE THEM.

Peer Response to Writing

As noted earlier, peer assessments work best when students are taught how to use them. The test of the effectiveness of the teaching is the quality of the peer feedback. Peer response is a reciprocal writing process designed so that students learn as much from giving feedback as they do from getting feedback (MacArthur, 2013). Writing researcher Jay Simmons analyzed peer feedback and responses about writing and found that in too many classrooms the majority were comprised of global praise (*Great job!*) and micro-edits (e.g., circling misspelled words). More skilled peer responders spent more time offering text feedback about the organization and concepts, as well the writer's craft ("You might consider using this at the beginning."). Simmons advises that "responders are taught, not born" (2003, p. 684) and that the best way to teach students to do it well is to share one's own writing and allowing students to respond to it. Teaching the difference between global, micro, and worthwhile feedback is also important. This is another value of providing rubrics to guide the feedback. Sometimes ask the peer to comment or rate the feedback or better, to write a note to the peer saying what they learnt and valued from the feedback can help improve the quality of the peer assessment. This practice enables students to become more skilled in responding rather than evaluating. Figure 25 includes a list of techniques for teaching students how to respond to one another's writing.

 TECHNIQUES FOR PEER RESPONSE

Technique	What the Teacher Does	What Students Do
Sharing your writing	Shares a piece of writing and asks for response Shares rewrites tied to class response	Offers comments in the teacher's writing
Clarifying evaluation vs. response	Shows evaluation is of product Response is to the writer	Understand that response is personable and helpful
Modeling specific praise	Shows how to tell what you like	Understand that cheerleading as a reader is too general to be helpful
Modeling understanding	Shows how to tell what you understood the piece to be about	Understand that reflecting back the piece to the writer is helpful
Modeling questions	Shows how to ask questions about what you didn't understand	Understand that questions related to the writer's purpose are helpful
Modeling suggestions	Shows how to suggest writing techniques	Understand that a responder leaves a writer knowing what to do next
Whole class response	Moderates response by class to one classmate's piece	Offer response Hear the response of others Hear what the writer finds helpful
Partner response	Pairs up students in class to respond to pieces	Practice response learned in whole-class session
Comment review	Reads the comments of peers to writers Suggests better techniques Devises minilessons	Get teacher feedback on comments
Response conference	Speaks individually with students responding inappropriately	Have techniques reinforced

Source: Simmons, J. (2003). Responders are taught, not born. *Journal of Adolescent and Adult Literacy, 46,* p. 690. Used with permission.

The notion that the teacher alone is the engine for revising is a false one that reinforces the misplaced belief that they are the only audience. Developing a sense of audience is an essential aspect of writing, yet in most classes we don't provide audiences for students to write to (Fisher, Frey, & Akhavan, 2018). Peer response provides writers with a knowledgeable audience that can assist them in shaping their revision.

Third grade teacher Jessica Harris has been utilizing peer response to writing in her distance learning class since the beginning of the school year. "I used it last year for the first time when we were in a face-to-face classroom. I had a lot of success and wanted to bring that forward this year in my distance learning work." Ms. Harris noted that she wants her students to be prepared across platforms, as it is likely that her school district will be moving to a hybrid model at some point. "Even then, we'll still need to use physical distancing. By teaching them how to do this virtually, I can have students in the classroom interact with those who are learning remotely."

Using the framework described by Simmons (2003), she has been modeling for her students three categories of responses that are useful for their fellow writers:

➡ **Playback the text** for the writer by briefly summarizing the main points as you understood them.

➡ **Discuss the reader's needs** by alerting the writer to confusions you had as you read the piece.

➡ **Identify writer's techniques** you noticed, such as the use of headings, examples, and direct quotes.

"I don't want them to get hung up on typing, so I have digital stickers for them to apply to the other person's writing: PT, RN, and WT," said Ms. Harris. "They read each other's work asynchronously and put their stickers on the document. When I have them in class, they go into breakout rooms to discuss their feedback. I move around between the breakout rooms to listen in and assess what's happening. They really listen to each other and their writing has really improved. This is something I'll take back to the classroom and use forever."

Peer-Assisted Reflection

Learning is a social act, as we learn in the company of other humans. Even in digital spaces, virtual contact with others is vital. The opportunity to speak or write can serve as a means to clarify one's own thinking about a topic. How often have you experienced a heightened sense of your own knowledge even as you were in the process of explaining it to someone else? This restructuring of one's own thinking is called cognitive elaboration, and results when learners explain ideas to each other and discuss any gaps in their understanding (Stegmann, Wecker, Weinberger, & Fischer, 2012).

Amanda Tremblay uses Peer-Assisted Reflection (PAR) with her high school math students (Reinholz, 2018). The theoretical underpinning of PAR is that there are differences between novices and mathematicians in how they approach difficult problems. While novices hastily identify one tool and then use it exclusively until the bitter end of the calculations, mathematicians use iterative processes that include analyzing, exploring, planning, implementing, and verifying (Schoenfeld, 1992). Students in Ms. Tremblay's classes complete an identified homework problem as a PAR problem, which requires that students write their reasoning as well as the calculations and solution, then send it to a partner the following day during live instruction. Ms. Tremblay moves the partners into breakout rooms, save for one group she keeps with her in the main room. This allows her to observe how the process is working and what might need to be retaught about the process.

Each partner examines the work their peer completed and annotates feedback about processes or solutions. This process typically takes about ten minutes, at which point the students receive their original paper back, now annotated with new ideas. The teams then discuss the feedback, and then make any corrections needed before submitting it. Providing a structured process for digital conversations that require cognitive elaboration on the part of learners has proved promising (Stegmann et al., 2012).

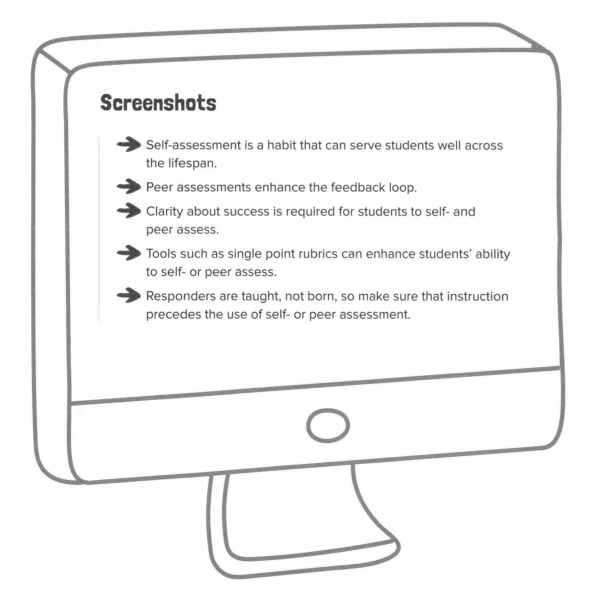

Screenshots

➡ Self-assessment is a habit that can serve students well across the lifespan.

➡ Peer assessments enhance the feedback loop.

➡ Clarity about success is required for students to self- and peer assess.

➡ Tools such as single point rubrics can enhance students' ability to self- or peer assess.

➡ Responders are taught, not born, so make sure that instruction precedes the use of self- or peer assessment.

3 ASSESSMENT UPGRADES

The operating system used by your computer or phone is probably not the same system as last year or the year before. We upgrade our systems on a regular basis as new learning is accumulated and new features are discovered. The same is true when we assess students' learning. There are a number of ways to document learning and use that information as feedback about our impact. Of course, like any upgrade, it's based on a system that is already in place. You have tools that you have used to document students' learning and to evaluate proficiency. Some of these will work perfectly well from a distance; others will not. We hope that these upgrades stick with you for a long time and that you'll continue to refine your assessment practices over time.

In this section:

- ☐ PERFORMANCE ASSESSMENTS
- ☐ IPSATIVE ASSESSMENTS
- ☐ CONFIRMATIVE ASSESSMENTS
- ☐ THINK LIKE AN EVALUATOR

UPGRADE 1: PERFORMANCE ASSESSMENTS

THE LEARNING STUDENTS DO MATTERS MORE WHEN WE TAKE RELEVANCE INTO ACCOUNT, AND ASSESSMENT IS A PART OF THAT LEARNING.

Some of our fondest memories of school were when we engaged in projects that let us apply what we had been learning to our own lives. Going deeper via these activities that excited us and fueled our love for learning. As teachers, it can be difficult to consistently engage our learners. After all, how many times have we heard: *When am I actually going to use this in real life?* (Nancy remembers saying that in high school about exponential functions. Discussions of "flattening the curve" in a pandemic changed that.) While that statement can drive us crazy, we recognize the truth underneath it. There's a demand for relevance, and that's on us. The learning students do matters more when we take relevance into account, and assessment is a part of that learning. This upgrade is intended to demonstrate relevance through the power of posing a simple question: *How do you make this knowledge your own?* We can ignite the thrill of learning in our students, regardless of the learning environment we are in.

Transfer of Knowledge

Students can demonstrate their mastery of a subject in a number of ways; that is the focus of this section. However, too often those demonstrations are limited to traditional test formats. While these have a place in your assessment toolkit, you will miss a lot as it narrows your view, and falsely tells students that only what is in the formal test is what matters.

Performance assessments provide students with a chance to apply more interdisciplinary concepts and skills. In other words, they are required to consolidate knowledge and thus promote transfer. That's a major goal of education: to apply what has been learned in new and novel ways. We want students to move from declarative knowledge (what it is), to procedural knowledge (how to use it), to conditional knowledge (when to use it) (Fisher, Frey, & Hattie, 2016). As John himself suggested in his 2014 Vernon Wall Lecture, learning can be defined as "[t]he process of developing sufficient surface knowledge to then move to deeper understanding such that one can appropriately transfer this learning to new tasks and situations."

Performance assessments are an important way in which students can demonstrate transfer through application to new and novel situations. An ongoing concern in remote learning is that the distance can make it more difficult to supervise and proctor traditional assessments. Performance assessments require students to draw on multiple skills and concepts and are pretty difficult to replicate. After all, it is unlikely that a debate performance, for instance, could be duplicated through nefarious means.

Panel Presentations

A tried and true method of ensuring students maintain accountability of their learning is to engage them in class presentations. While functional and applicable in both face-to-face and distance learning, this may not be especially engaging for all students. At its worst, the class (and you) are subjected to a seemingly endless procession of individual presentations that feel more like something to be endured than enjoyed. Definitely not inspiring! Part of the problem is the audience. Presenting to your peers and the teacher can seem like an echo chamber. Changing the audience can boost the relevancy of the project and in doing so improve your ability to assess.

Leverage the online community to find experts in the subject field that are willing to listen to your students. A silver lining of our current reality means that more people are working from home and may have time to tune into a video conference rather than physically make their way to the classroom. Whether this be a local politician, librarian, medical doctor, or activist, we can maximize distance learning communication tools to reach out to communities for assistance. Don't be afraid to ask parents! Many times, our parents can be our greatest resource, insofar as they themselves may be experts in a field of study. Students then prepare to present their project to a panel. Much of the process for student preparation is the same as in class presentations, the only thing we change is the audience. Presenting to real life people (outside of classmates) is a life skill students will need outside of the classroom.

Presenting to a panel increases the likelihood that our students will not only take the task more seriously but will engage in learning that extends outside of memorizing content (as they sometimes might for in-class presentations). The added rigor of presenting to a panel will encourage students to engage in deeper consolidation of learning. Fifth-grade teacher Ms. Alaba used a special guest to wrap up her Weather Watch unit—a weather forecaster from a local television station. Students each had two minutes to interpret a weather map and give the weather report for a region in the world. "I don't remember the last time I've seen my students take their presentations so seriously!" she noted. This is not the first time her students have engaged in panel presentations to members of her community. "It seems that people are genuinely excited to join our virtual class presentations. I have received more replies than I could have imagined! It has been a great learning experience having my students interact with members of their community."

It can be tough to reach out to the community if our network is small, and it can be a bit daunting cold calling or sending an email without any prior connection. Thankfully, there are organizations that seek to connect students from around the world. An example of one such group is *The Center for Global Education* (http://tcge.tiged.org/), which connects students to global issues through video conferencing.

> PERFORMANCE ASSESSMENTS PROVIDE STUDENTS WITH A CHANCE TO APPLY MORE INTERDISCIPLINARY CONCEPTS AND SKILLS.

Debates

Although not a new strategy, we would like to add debates to our upgrade list as an assessment where students can demonstrate their competence in a distance learning environment. Well-constructed debates can challenge students to consider the nuances of controversial topics, formulate arguments, and use formal reasoning (Zimmerman & Robertson, 2017). Formal discussion, such as debates and Socratic seminars, have an effect size of 0.82, indicating a strong potential for accelerating learning (Hattie, n.d.). The potential for students to engage in rich conversation and assessment of that conversation exists in distance learning debates, but there are some important considerations we must make to ensure authentic assessment occurs.

1. Debate procedures and structure must be explicitly taught and practiced with students.

2. A rubric for debate performance should be based on success criteria and can be co-constructed with students.

3. Students should be responsible for creating arguments for both sides of the debate. Teachers then assign debate teams on the day of the debate to allow time to craft arguments.

PERFORMANCE ASSESSMENTS ARE AN IMPORTANT WAY IN WHICH STUDENTS CAN DEMONSTRATE TRANSFER THROUGH APPLICATION TO NEW AND NOVEL SITUATIONS.

Debates in the distance learning classroom can be both synchronous or asynchronous in design. Synchronous debates could be done using a web-conferencing program, ensuring protocols and procedures are understood by all learners. Asynchronous debates can occur through virtual platforms, like Flipgrid (for video replies) or Kialo (structured written debates).

Howard Williamson, a high school world history teacher, has used TikTok as a means to engage in a historical debate. The TikTok platform, although designed to be used as social media, can provide a link between popular social media outlets and the distance learning classroom. Mr. Williamson notes that "students are limited by the 60 second maximum video length" and that "they were working with a platform they were already comfortable with." His history class engaged in debating the impact of Nationalism in 1930's Europe, and through their own historical lens students provided their own perspectives and debated the topic through a series of videos (all using the same hashtag). While we are not suggesting that all of us should use TikTok, we would like to take note that in this case the teacher leveraged a relevant social media tool to generate evidence of learning.

Socratic Seminar

Another way to engage students in a discussion without argumentation (debate) is to use a Socratic seminar. Israel (2002) describes the format as

> a formal discussion, based on a text, in which the leader asks open-ended questions. Within the context of the discussion, students listen closely to the comments of others, thinking critically for themselves, and articulate their own thoughts and their responses to the thoughts of others. They learn to work cooperatively and to question intelligently and civilly. (p. 89)

Socratic seminars allow students to engage with a text and topic meaningfully, take time to invest in critical thought, respond to both questions about a text and reflect on comments made by other students in the class. Because it is a text-based discussion, students should be aware that a Socratic seminar will be used when introducing the reading to ensure purposeful engagement with the text. The process is just as important as the product. In other words, a Socratic seminar provides you with an opportunity to assess a variety of elements, including oral language and speaking skills, application of critical thinking and reasoning, and comprehension of the target text. As with debates, the procedures and structure should be explicitly taught and practiced with students, including establishing your limited role as a facilitator of the seminar (see Roberts & Billings, 1999 for information about creating open-ended questions).

The tools used to engage in distance learning Socratic seminars are identical to those used for debates. The web conferencing tool you use is likely to be adequate. A Socratic seminar relies on a fishbowl structure, with a small group of students actively discussing while the others observe and take notes.

1. Host a small group of students in the main room for a discussion, while the other students observe the interaction.

2. After introducing the purpose and the topic, the teacher's role is primarily as an observer, interjecting only as needed to forward the discussion, usually by posing a new open question.

3. The inner circle of participants discusses the topic (the fishbowl), ask and answer questions to each other, while those in the outer circle listen.

4. A major art is for the teacher to NOT be seen as the source of answers or as the director of the Socratic discussions, and to restrain from asking closed questions (no matter how hard students try to bring the teacher in as the conductor!).

5. After the first round of discussion, members of the outer circle exchange places with those in the inner circle, and the discussion continues.

6. After all the students have participated in the inner circle, the teacher takes a more overt role in the discussion, asking questions that encourage students to synthesize their thinking.

7. Students are asked to comment on the process and their own learning. Often teachers provide language or sentence starters to help students respond to each other.

The assessment of student responses during a Socratic seminar will vary depending on the focus of the subject. Single-point rubrics based off of co-constructed success criteria can serve as a brilliant assessment of student learning. Another recommendation is to have the students engage in a reflective assessment of the process, with students considering the following:

➡ The degree to which text-centered talk dominated

➡ Student individual participation in the discussion

➡ The extent to which they grew in their understanding of the topic

Naturally, these types of reflections would be based on preestablished learning intentions and success criteria prior to the beginning of the Socratic seminar.

Research Projects

Clarise Ivy's Grade 4 language arts class is starting to work on a transdisciplinary research project that crosses with their social studies curriculum. Their project, "Literature of the Land" focuses on the driving question: *How does where I live influence what I read?* This challenges students to use their regional knowledge of Canada, where they live, and engage in finding story books from regions across Canada. Students have voice and choice over the region they choose, and from there they must use their research skills to find out more information from the area. When students were asked about their choice one explained, "I chose the province of Newfoundland, because my family is from there. I've never visited but I would like to learn more about it." Upon choosing a region, Ms. Ivy led the students through how to conduct proper research. "I modeled how to use Google to access local libraries and send inquiries about local children's books. We also spent time using Google Earth and Google Maps to ensure students had a grasp of the geography of Canada."

Upon learning more about regional story books and finding one of their choosing, students must create a book review along with a read aloud on Flipgrid. Students will be able to ask questions and engage in learning about regional stories from across Canada. When Ms. Ivy was asked what she hopes this project will inspire her students to do, she replied, "I hope this inspires my students to choose books that are from other places and recognize the uniqueness that exists in all parts of Canada."

There were some important elements in Ms. Ivy's conceptualization of this project, conducted in a distance learning environment, and these transcend face-to-face and virtual instruction. The first is that she used a driving conceptual question to encourage a richer exploration of content. The second is that she modeled how to engage in their online research, an especially vital step in younger grades. The third element is that she kept the taking action aspect of the project in mind by asking herself, *what will this inspire my students to do?* We can build research projects that excite the thrill of learning for our students.

Flexible Assessment Through Relevance and Choice

IF RELEVANCE IS THE ENGINE TO LEARNING, THEN INVITING STUDENTS TO MAKE CHOICES AMONG VARIOUS OPTIONS CAN INCREASE THE RELEVANCE OF PERFORMANCE ASSESSMENTS.

If relevance is the engine to learning, then inviting students to make choices among various options can increase the relevance of performance assessments. There are times when relevance is baked right into the assessment. For example, successfully completing a performance assessment in driving leads to a permit or license. In many career and technical education courses, there are typically licensing requirements that students complete through demonstration of skill. But unless you're a driver education or CTE teacher, you're probably not teaching content that is directly related to a license or certificate. For most educators, relevance comes through making explicit associations between the content and its application inside and outside of the classroom. Educators can articulate the relevance of learning across three dimensions (Frey, Hattie, & Fisher, 2018).

The first is application in their own lives, while the second is to involve the student directly by asking them about their concerns. The third is to note the value of becoming an educated member of the community.

➡ *Application in their own lives:* Why are we learning about syllables? So we can spell big words.

➡ **Direct student involvement**: Why are we learning about the civil rights movement? Because understanding past actions prepare us to be social justice advocates for vulnerable people in our community.

➡ **An educated member of the community**: Why are we learning the scientific method? So we can participate in a science-literate society.

Relevance is more than just being familiar; it is about being authentic. There's a popular meme that says, "Math: The only place where people buy 60 watermelons and no one asks why." Indeed. Simply adding watermelons, or candy, or some other familiar object to a math word problem doesn't actually make it relevant.

A second driver of relevance is choice. And it's not just choice for the sake of choice but more a choice between options. We are not advocating students choose their adventure, as when all of us begin learning many topics, we do not know what we do not know. And some students thrive on challenge and are prepared to make choices to learn that which they do not yet know, and others who are fearful of challenge or just want "to do their best" choose that which they can already do and once again, fall behind those venturing into new learning. The choice we offer should be from various options, provided all options can lead efficiently and effectively toward the success criteria. Such choice allows students to articulate the relevance of learning for themselves. As educators of young people, we are on a continuous journey with them to build their internal motivations for learning. Intrinsic motivation, which is fueled by student choice, is associated with higher levels of student effort and performance (Patall, Cooper, & Robinson, 2008). Their meta-analysis of forty-one studies found that between two and four choices worked best for children to make decisions.

Choice can and should be a feature in some assessment opportunities. Flexible assessments are those that allow students to make choices about how they will be assessed. The purpose of a flexible assessment can vary. Choice can be used as part of assessment *as* learning, especially in providing students with opportunities to select an activity or project to help them set goals for themselves, such as choosing two physical fitness tests to measure their current fitness level. Alternatively, they can exercise choice within the larger process of assessment *for* learning in their movement toward unit goals. As an example, a student might select three math word problems from a bank of five possible items to apply a newly learned computational skill during asynchronous learning. In other cases, a student might propose how to demonstrate their knowledge. Finally, assessment *of* learning, which is used to make judgments of student performance, can be offered as a choice of three possible final projects in an instructional unit.

For example, history teacher Joanna Schaefer asked her students to compose letters to elected officials about issues that mattered to them. They had to research topics and write short essays as well as compose a letter to a politician. As an example, Yons wrote to a state senator about unemployment (see Figure 26) whereas Frida wrote to a US congressperson and Mauricio wrote to the local mayor. The research and letters were not optional, but the topics and the audience were.

26 LETTER TO STATE SENATOR

October 14, 2020

Dear Senator,

My name is Yons Said and I am 16 years old. I am a student at Health Sciences High and live in San Diego, CA. I am writing to you today to address the unemployment problem in the United States which is a really important issue to me personally as well as our country.

In 2020, the unemployment rates in America spiked to 14.7% from a recent low of 3.5% in February. A lot of this recent spike can be attributed to COVID-19. San Diego is being negatively impacted by the loss of jobs due to the pandemic. Personally, I know a few people with large families are struggling with rent and bills, even with the government-issued unemployment benefits (CARES Act). I believe that with the unusual circumstances of COVID-19, the government should provide additional support to the people.

After researching your position on unemployment, I found that you also feel similarly to me. I've seen in an article that you've stated, "Oh, look at the unemployment numbers. Yeah, okay. People are working, and guess what, they're working two and three jobs to pay the bills. The economy is not working for working people." Clearly, you believe that the everyday man isn't protected in today's economy. I feel that if the economy is not tailored toward common people, then the government should be the protection and assistance for them.

Quite frankly, the current unemployment benefits aren't enough for a lot of large, immigrant families. I urge you to address this issue publicly, which will cause media coverage about this problem. By addressing the unemployment issues large families are facing, we would be shining a light on a rather overlooked part of California.

Sincerely,

Yons Said
HSHMC Inc.
3910 University Ave #100
San Diego, CA 92105

Kindergarten teacher Malena Leyva offered choice boards for her students in their distance learning math class. Her assessments are often a combination of individually administered ones to determine specific skills, and flexible assessments that provide each child a choice. "Families appreciate the fact that their child can complete a math assessment in a variety of ways. I try to create choices that involve common objects in the house," said Ms. Leyva. As part of their study of whole numbers, the teacher needed to assess how her students were generalizing their knowledge of counting and cardinality. She provided families with a list of possible ways for their child to demonstrate their ability to write numbers and compare them to one another, asking each child to select one from the list. She asked them to compare the numbers 6 and 3. She recorded her directions, saying, "Line up 6 objects that are the same in your house, and

3 other objects that are the same. Write each number and tell me how many of each, which one is more, and which one is less."

➔ You can take two pictures showing each, along with the numbers.

➔ You can make a Flipgrid video explaining each number.

➔ You can show me your work in a live conference session with me.

"The formats can be challenging, and I want to make sure that I am offering several different ways they can show me what they know," said the teacher. "Using a more flexible assessment approach is something I know the families appreciate."

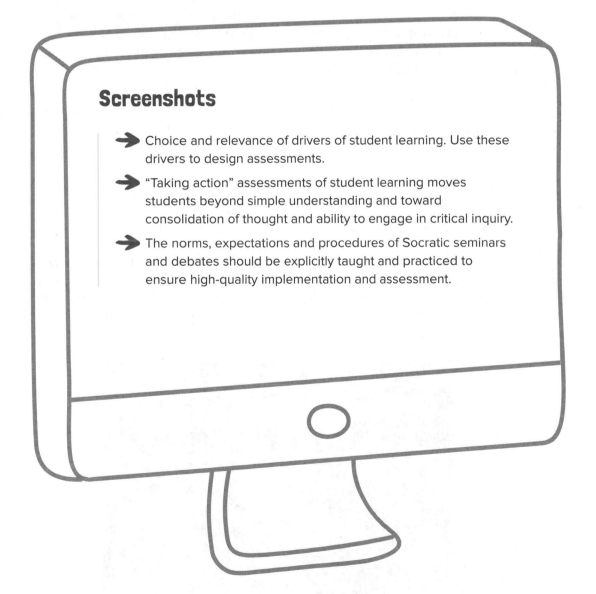

Screenshots

➔ Choice and relevance of drivers of student learning. Use these drivers to design assessments.

➔ "Taking action" assessments of student learning moves students beyond simple understanding and toward consolidation of thought and ability to engage in critical inquiry.

➔ The norms, expectations and procedures of Socratic seminars and debates should be explicitly taught and practiced to ensure high-quality implementation and assessment.

UPGRADE 2: IPSATIVE ASSESSMENTS

Grace Kao's Grade 6 English students are approaching the end of the first quarter of the school year, and it is time to look back on the growth her students have made. They are a key part of this process. In the first week of school, Ms. Kao had her students set reading and writing goals for themselves. In the weeks since then, her students have engaged in lots of writing assignments of varying lengths for a variety of purposes. The writing rubrics they have used have been consistent and drawn from her state's writing rubrics. They vary only inasmuch as they are for narrative, informational, or argumentation purposes. She has scored their writing assignments throughout. Now she is asking them to compare their work from the beginning and end of the quarter.

"We've been doing a lot of informational writing this quarter. Take out your scored writing from the second week. That piece was on advice for getting good grades in school. The second one was from last week when you wrote about the life of one of the authors we've read," says Ms. Kao. Using the form in Figure 27, students replicated the scores they received from the two essays so they could compare the two.

"Now that you've put the data together, I'd like for you to write your impressions. This is a fifteen-minute timed writing that you'll do right now," said Ms. Kao. "There are four questions to answer, and I'll keep them displayed to help you address each."

➡ Where are you seeing growth?

➡ What is still a challenge?

➡ What surprised you?

➡ How will you meet your goal for next quarter?

The English teacher uses her students' comparative essay reflections to inform the comments she writes as part of their report cards. She is mindful that her role is not only to report mastery but also to report progress, noting that a single-letter grade conveys little to the student or the family about progress. The comparative essay, inspired by Ferlazzo's (2010) work with his high school students, is an example of an ipsative assessment.

istock/eclipse_images

Leverage the video skills of your students by asking them to create monthly videos about themselves.

27 COMPARATIVE SELF-ASSESSMENT FOR INFORMATIONAL WRITING IN GRADE 6

Title and Date of First Essay	Title and Date of Second Essay
Organization/Purpose	
Topic is introduced clearly to preview what is to follow 4 3 2 1	Topic is introduced clearly to preview what is to follow 4 3 2 1
Ideas and concepts are organized using definition, classification, or compare/contrast 4 3 2 1	Ideas and concepts are organized using definition, classification, or compare/contrast 4 3 2 1
Transitions create cohesion and show relationships among ideas 4 3 2 1	Transitions create cohesion and show relationships among ideas 4 3 2 1
A concluding statement supports the explanation given 4 3 2 1	A concluding statement supports the explanation given 4 3 2 1
Task, purpose, and audience are aligned to prompt 4 3 2 1	Task, purpose, and audience are aligned to prompt 4 3 2 1
Evidence/Elaboration	
Develops the topic with relevant facts, definitions, details, and examples 4 3 2 1	Develops the topic with relevant facts, definitions, details, and examples 4 3 2 1
Follows a standard format for citations 4 3 2 1	Follows a standard format for citations 4 3 2 1
Skillfully quotes and paraphrases 4 3 2 1	Skillfully quotes and paraphrases 4 3 2 1
Uses relevant information from multiple sources 4 3 2 1	Uses relevant information from multiple sources 4 3 2 1
Effective and appropriate style enhances content 4 3 2 1	Effective and appropriate style enhances content 4 3 2 1
Conventions	
Demonstrates grade-level grammar, usage, and conventions 4 3 2 1	Demonstrates grade-level grammar, usage, and conventions 4 3 2 1

Ipsative Assessments

Although the term is not widely used in education, the practice is. Ipsative assessments compare a student's present performance to past performance (Isaacs, Zara, Herbert, Coombs, & Smith, 2013). These can be done by the teacher, for example, comparing initial assessment and final assessment data to measure one's impact of teaching. This process will be explained in more detail in the final upgrade on using Visible Learning tools to determine effect-size impact. In this upgrade, the focus is on more direct student involvement in the process.

We do this all the time as adults. We track our weight and other health markers, compare gas mileage in different driving conditions, monitor our weekly screen time, and examine our monthly budget this year compared to last. In all of these cases, time is a factor, but so is what we do with the data. Your health-marker trends might signal that you need to exercise more and eat less. You might adjust your driving habits, reel in the amount of screen time you've been getting, or make some decisions that will positively impact your budget. In other words, you set goals and take action.

Student involvement in ipsative assessment can prompt similar effects for students. These practices are assessment *as* learning, as students gain insight into their progress and areas of challenge and set goals for themselves.

> IPSATIVE ASSESSMENTS COMPARE A STUDENT'S PRESENT PERFORMANCE TO PAST PERFORMANCE.

Goal-Setting Conferences

With an effect size of 0.51, clear goal intentions have the potential to accelerate student learning (Hattie, n.d.). During a time when there is concern over potential decline in student learning, acceleration techniques are exactly what is needed to bridge gaps. The goal alone isn't enough; there must be intention that goes with it. Think of a goal setting conference with a student as an if-then plan (Gollwitzer, 1999). However, the goals can't belong to someone else—they need student ownership. Characteristics of goals that motivate students include the following (Nordengren, 2019):

➡ Building competence

➡ Providing autonomy and choice

➡ Aligning with the student's interests

➡ Changing how they perceive themselves (perhaps the most important of all)

Steer goals away from performance ones ("I want to get all 4s on the next writing rubric.") and toward mastery goals ("I want my written explanations to be clear to other readers.").

That's what ninth-grade advisor Jonathan Yates has been doing with his mentees this year. When the school moved into distance learning, the staff recognized that keeping in close contact with every student would be more important than ever. Every adult in the school, certificated and classified, has about ten students to keep in contact with on their roster for the year. Mr. Yates is a teaching assistant at the school. He meets with his group as part of their scheduled classes to build relationships, provide emotional check-ins, and help students set goals.

Mr. Yates and his colleagues use a six-week goal-setting cycle with students to keep goals attainable. "Right now, long-term goals are challenging for them," he said of his students. The group discusses short-term goals in two areas: content learning goals and personal learning goals. Mr. Yates sets up their goals on a collaborative spreadsheet so that students can see each other's goals and to create a network of encouragers. The second column of the spreadsheet targets intentions by asking them to identify how they will achieve it. Salwa stated that a goal was to master polynomials, a topic that was giving her trouble in algebra. To do so, she admitted that she "needed to start attending office hours" with her math teacher, an option that she had so far not done. In the subsequent weeks, one of the activities during advisory is a roundtable check-in on goals. Mr. Yates records their efforts on the document, indicating whether it was done or not. Salwa initially had a slow start but soon got into the rhythm of going to office hours for additional support. At the six-week mark, each student had an opportunity to revisit their goals and compare them to their efforts, intentions, and outcomes. Salwa couldn't wait for her turn to tell the group that she had passed the latest math competency, of which polynomials was a major focus. Mr. Yates brought the conversation back to what she had done to meet her goals. "I also share this information with their content teachers, so that they're aware of the goals and the intentions their students have for their classes."

THE GOALS CAN'T BELONG TO SOMEONE ELSE— THEY NEED STUDENT OWNERSHIP.

Video Diaries

Distance and blended learning platforms have fostered a rapid rise in the capacity of students, even very young ones, to create and view their own videos. Leverage the video skills of your students by asking them to create monthly videos about themselves and then revisit these videos throughout the school year. You can pose a different question each month for the topic. Fourth-grade teacher Nathan Rafferty asked these questions of his students each month (see Figure 28). Some of his questions are related

28 MONTHLY VIDEO DIARY QUESTIONS

Month	Video Diary Questions
September	What are your aspirations for this school year? How will you know you have met them?
October	We've been studying about our region's history this month. What would you tell a new neighbor about our region?
	Reflection: Watch your previous entry before answering this question: How are you changing physically, emotionally, or academically? What is the same?
November	When you have a hard decision to make, who do you turn to?
	Reflection: Watch your previous entries before answering this question: How are you changing physically, emotionally, or academically? What is the same?
December	When did you use math this week outside of the classroom?
	Reflection: Watch your previous entries before answering this question: How are you changing physically, emotionally, or academically? What is the same?

(Continued)

(Continued)

Month	Video Diary Questions
January	**What responsibilities come with freedom?** *Reflection:* Watch your previous entries before answering this question: How are you changing physically, emotionally, or academically? What is the same?
February	**What do other people like about you?** *Reflection:* Watch your previous entries before answering this question: How are you changing physically, emotionally, or academically? What is the same?
March	**We've been learning about sound waves this month. How would you explain how sound travels to someone else?** *Reflection:* Watch your previous entries before answering this question: How are you changing physically, emotionally, or academically? What is the same?
April	**Why do we need rules?** *Reflection:* Watch your previous entries before answering this question: How are you changing physically, emotionally, or academically? What is the same?
May	**What advice do you have for third graders to be successful next year?** *Reflection:* Watch your previous entries before answering this question: How are you changing physically, emotionally, or academically? What is the same?

to their content learning, while other questions are about themselves. "I want to make sure that I'm asking them questions that allow them to show what they know about themselves and the world," said Mr. Rafferty.

These video diary entries provide him with another glimpse of who they are as individuals, something he prizes even more in distance learning. "I used to have them write monthly, but it has been great to view these as they talk out their ideas," said the teacher. However, the video diaries, although useful for him, are of even more value to his students, who watch their previous entries before recording the next one. Beginning in the second month of school, he asks them to watch the previous entries and reflect on changes they are noticing about themselves, as well as what is the same. "Children at this age are becoming more self-conscious, and that can be a two-edged sword. I want them to be comfortable with themselves and know that change is a part of growing up." He has found these video diaries to be invaluable in conferences with parents, too. Mr. Yates continued. "Sometimes these can be useful for broaching difficult topics, as well as for celebrating the progress they are making as a young person."

Portfolios

As students navigate their way through their classes, they naturally gather assessments that provide a snapshot in time about their learning. By combining their accumulation of knowledge and skills into a culminating activity, we can create a summary of student progress over the course of a year. After all, if we truly want to create the most authentic assessment possible for our students, we must consider that learning should not be measured by what we do or what we know in a moment, but rather on how we perform using information we have learned.

Consider student portfolios as an evaluation of learning. Student portfolios of learning are one strategy for the evaluation of student learning over time. There are many types of portfolios, but we will discuss assessment portfolios, which are used to document the progression of student learning over time (Danielson & Abrutyn, 1997). The strength of an assessment portfolio is that it can demonstrate growth over time, rather than achievement in the moment, as is the case with some exams. Teachers often shy away from the portfolio assessments due to the complexity and time it takes to both build and assess. We acknowledge that it is a time-consuming assessment to both, but consider the following advantages it can offer:

➡ Portfolios show student growth over time.

➡ Portfolios involve students in the evaluation of their own learning.

➡ Portfolios reflect the process of learning against an outcome, not simply knowledge of an outcome.

➡ Portfolios demonstrate interconnected thought processes and can leverage trans disciplinary subjects.

➡ Portfolio assessment may reveal instructional gaps (assessment *for* learning).

➡ Evaluation of portfolios can be both holistic and specific in their assessment.

Portfolio assessments have the potential to glean deep levels of thinking processes from our students. Not only that, but as students navigate their way through these portfolios they can monitor and adjust based on feedback from peers and teachers. When done correctly, it can become the perfect cumulating activity for distance learning students.

Formative Practice Tests

The name given by researchers to this approach highlights the challenge of the dichotomy between formative and summative assessments. Most people would suggest that tests are summative, but in this case, they are used formatively. There are a number of studies and meta-analyses that suggest that formative practice tests are useful in improving learning (e.g., Adesope, Trevisan, & Sundararajan, 2017). We locate them in the self-assessment playlist because they are powerful ways for students to analyze their current performance and then take action to close the gap between what they know and what they still need to learn.

The major mistake in this thinking is using the term *assessment* with formative and summative as too often it puts major onus on the test. When the terms were first invented by Michael Scriven, he used formative and summative evaluation—as he wanted the emphasis on the use of evaluative information during or at the end of a sequence, intervention, or program. Both formative and summative interpretations can be most worthwhile, but the emphasis can be different. Formative evaluation emphasizes collecting evidence to make interpretations to improve the learning while it is still underway, and summative evaluation emphasizes collecting evidence to make interpretations at the end to review success or otherwise in teaching and learning.

Essentially, formative practice testing requires that teachers provide students a practice version of an assessment several days in advance of the "real" test. This is not an initial assessment before the unit of instruction begins. Initial assessments allow teachers to determine what students already know so that they can focus instruction on what students still need to know.

Practice testing provides students an opportunity to reflect on their performance and take action. Practice tests, paired with feedback, enhance learning. Formative practice tests are much more effective than a study guide. After all, we are very likely to spend more time studying things that we already know rather than things we don't know. Practice tests allow students to focus their review and extend their understanding. Importantly, one practice test is usually sufficient. As the saying goes, "You don't fatten sheep by weighing them." The evidence also suggests that practice tests are effective in elementary or secondary schools.

The format of the practice test can vary: multiple choice, constructed response, dichotomous choices such as true and false, and essays all work. The practice test should not be the exact test that will be administered later but the topics and level of complexity should be consistent. In physical school, practice testing is fairly rare as teachers are concerned about the use of time. Every assessment administered reduces the amount of time for instruction. That's the way physical school works. There are minutes devoted to specific topics and subjects, and they become precious. But in distance learning, students can complete and analyze practice tests during asynchronous learning.

THE KEY TO FORMATIVE PRACTICE TESTING IS TO GET STUDENTS TO INTERPRET THE RESULTS.

The key to formative practice testing is to get students to interpret the results. It's their quality interpretations that matter most. There are a number of ways to have students analyze their results. In doing so, they identify areas that need their attention as well as areas that they have mastered. They may need more instruction or more practice and knowing the difference can motivate students to participate in additional learning opportunities.

For example, the students in Matt Oliveros's second-grade class were learning about regular and irregular verb tenses. Using a feature in Seesaw, students sorted words into categories: past, present, and future. They then checked their answers and identified any words that they placed incorrectly. They made a list of the words that were incorrect and recorded a message to their teacher about the words they missed and why they thought they missed them. Mr. Oliveros provided students with additional instruction based on the patterns of errors his students experienced.

In Jacob Hill's sixth-grade class, students were studying ancient Egypt. Mr. Hill identified the complexity of each question, noting that some of the questions were more foundational and some were more complex. He gave his students a practice test four days before the "real" test and students analyzed their results. Of course, students could search the internet for answers to most of these questions, but they don't because he talks with them about "knowing what you still need to learn." In addition, for the graded tests, Mr. Hill interviews his students using random questions from the test to check on their understandings. As he says, "This is not gotcha, but rather about learning academic honesty and the value in knowing what you know and what you still need to know." He added, "I use some tests but there are a lot of other ways that I use to determine students' understanding. Tests are just one way for them to think about the information in our class." Mr. Hill's students use the tool in Figure 29, shared with them as a Google Slide.

29  **ANALYSIS OF PRACTICE TEST**

Complex Items I Got Wrong		Complex Items I Got Right	
Foundational Items I Got Wrong		**Foundational Items I Got Right**	
What did I do well?	**What do I need to practice?**	**What do I need Mr. Hill to teach me?**	

Screenshots

➔ Ipsative assessments encourage students to consider their past and present learning, set goals, and monitor their progress. Consider these assessments *as* learning opportunities because students gain new insights about themselves.

➔ Digital portfolios eliminate the storage factors that have caused teachers to avoid their use. Keep the three *Rs* in mind for assessment portfolios: representation, reflection, and revision.

➔ Practice tests allow students the opportunity to engage in mastery before evaluation. Generally, the view of an evaluation of learning is that once a student has completed their assessment, the learning stops.

UPGRADE 3: CONFIRMATIVE ASSESSMENTS

There are some assessments that are used to confirm students' proficiency with the learning expectations or standards. This can be short term or long term. In some cases, the assessment comes at the end of the semester or year and other times at the end of an extensive unit of instruction. In the purist sense, confirmative evaluation is the process of "collecting, examining, and interpreting data and information in order to determine the continuing competence of learners or the continuing effectiveness of instructional materials" (Hellebrandt & Russell, 1993).

The definition of continuing competence varies in terms of time and tools. The question is, how long after instruction should we assess students to determine if they have learned something. The Ebbinghaus Forgetting Curve (1885) shows that information is lost over time when there is no effort to use it or retain it. More currently, people think of the strength of memory, which refers to the memory traces that are created in the brain. The stronger the memory is, or the more it is accessed, the more likely one is to be able to recall the specific information. Our colleague Joseph has argued that mastery requires maintenance and requires that students continue to use and demonstrate skills long after he has taught them.

The tools used to determine continuing competence are also up for discussion. Is one assessment enough? What types of assessment are more effective to confirm that students know, understand, or can do something? In this upgrade, we'll focus on a few tools that teachers can use in their attempts to confirm students' understanding. As a cautionary note, some of the tools used in confirmative assessments are criticized as promoting rote memorization and preventing critical thinking and analysis. To be sure, there are poorly constructed multiple-choice tests and poorly worded essay prompts. But there are bad examples of a wide range of assessment types, including project-based learning and performance assessment. Xu, Kauer, and Tupy (2016) note that there are ways to improve the quality of assessment items including those on multiple-choice tests such that they are useful in providing information to students and their teachers. As you have read through this book, we hope you noted that we believe teachers should be assessing learning often and making informed decisions about what to do with the information. Confirmative assessments are part of the overall assessment system, not the one and only tool we use.

Multiple-Choice Tests

Using multiple-choice examinations in the distance learning environment can prove to be challenging, especially when these exams are typically given in a secured environment. Thankfully, there are a multitude of online proctoring programs that administer exams in a secured environment (Socrative, ProctorU, Examsoft, etc.). Yet what we found alarming is when we conducted an internet search about proctoring programs, the most commonly searched question was "*How can you cheat on proctored exams?*" There are even articles written about the best ways to cheat on these exams!

We have to wonder about how to maintain assessments that are as accurate as possible in distance learning. The truth is, we will never be able to know for sure if our students are cheating on these exams. It comes down to trust. We have to trust that students are not going to cheat. And it helps by your demonstrating to the students that the stakes are high because you and they can learn from the test, gain feedback about where to move next in teaching and learning, and it is valuable to complete these tests for these reasons. But the more it is high-stakes testing for final grades, the story can change. Of course, we cannot hinge our assessment practices solely on trust, but we do need to consider the construction of our exams. Think back to Assessment Cookie 7, Everything Is Searchable, So Plan Accordingly. If our students can find responses to our multiple-choice assessments online, there is a chance the questions may not drive students to deeper levels of thinking.

Department chair Frank Spilak must consider the implications of administering secured exams in a distance learning environment. He suggests ensuring there is a balance of tests and examinations with qualitative assessments. His department firmly believes in the triangulation of data and evidence when it comes to student assessment. As such, his teachers engage in post exam conferences with each individual student. These post exam conferences are intended as an informal reflection on student performance in the exam. Mr. Spilak's team uses this time with the student to make an accurate determination as to whether the student completed the exam with integrity and honesty. Mr. Spilak calls these interviews a "second check for understanding." The three components of his department's "triangulation of evaluation" are multiple-choice exam, essay or other product, and post-assessment interview. Taken together, these can provide a more accurate evaluation of student learning that occurred over a unit of study.

If a multiple-choice assessment is nonnegotiable in your learning environment, we suggest applying some of the below shifts to encourage students into a deeper consolidation of knowledge in answering the questions.

Here is some advice from distance learning educators who use multiple-choice exams:

1. **Reduce the number of questions and increase the complexity.** Many multiple-choice assessments have a significant number of questions that test basic recall and memorization. In other words, things that can be searched on the internet. Seek to decrease the number of these questions and create questions in which students must apply higher-order thinking skills to correctly answer the question.

   - In humanities courses, questions could be based on a passage or a prompt where students must make reasoned judgments before answering a question.

   - In mathematics, questions would encourage students to solve a multistep equation, before choosing the correct response.

   - In science, questions could have the students analyze scientific data prior to answering a question.

Essentially the goal of reframing our thinking around multiple-choice exams in distance learning is to remove the ability for students to cheat to get the answer.

2. **Create questions where students will have to justify their response.**
    A simple strategy to reduce a potential exam security breach would be to have students justify their response on the multiple-choice exam. Along with a multiple-choice answer sheet, students will also have to complete a response justification form (see Figure 30). The QR code will also take you to a sample Google Doc of the form. We can choose to have students justify their response for all questions or a selection. Naturally that decision is up to the classroom teacher. By having students complete these forms along with their answers, we can gain more insight into their understanding of the assessment. This strategy can also create an equitable platform for our students who struggle with multiple-choice exams. Oftentimes we find our students understand the content, and skills that are required to perform well on an assessment, but they end up getting a wrong answer. The justification of their answers can give us insight into their thought process as they were answering the question. Just like that our evaluation of learning can become an assessment *for* learning.

Scan this QR code to view a sample exam justification form.

30 **RESPONSE JUSTIFICATION FORM**

Name: _____

Date: _____

Exam Title: _____

Question	Response
Justification for response chosen:	

3. **Provide opportunities for students to tell you what else they know.** Years ago, some teachers started adding a page at the end of the test that simply said "Write an explanation of everything else you know about this topic that was not on the test. I'll review it and add to your overall score." Reports are that students thrived with this opportunity and demonstrated additional knowledge and skills that impressed their teachers. As a chemistry teacher said, "I was really impressed with all the things they learned in the unit that I hadn't included on the test. It showed me that they were really focused on some aspects more than others. Great learning for me." In distance learning, we're seeing some teachers give a multiple-choice test and telling students that they must complete the test with a good effort, even though the answers won't count toward their grade. Their grade, their teacher tells them, will be based on their description of their learning, which they are asked to write at the end of the test. Why make them take the multiple-choice test if it doesn't count? One teacher said, "I am trying to build habits with my students. They will encounter these tests in their future and need that skill. When I told them their scores on the multiple-choice section did not count, but that I would review their answers, I think that they all took it without searching the internet. I got a chance to really see what they understood. And they ended up using information within the test, because they really read it, to compose their summary of learning.

Other Formats for Tests

Of course, there are a number of other formats for test items, including constructed response, short answer, and dichotomous choices such as true/false. As McAllister and Guidice (2012) noted, true/false is considered "one of the most unreliable forms of assessment" (p. 195) so we won't spend time on that, even though they are very easy to grade. Short answer questions, such as fill in the blank, are open ended and require that students produce the answer rather than select from a range of options. Thus, students cannot guess the answer. These items are usually used for assessing knowledge rather than the application of information. They are relatively easy to grade but do not provide a comprehensive view of students understanding of the content. According to Oosterhof, Conrad, & Ely (2008, p. 88), it is important to keep the following criteria in mind when writing short answer completion questions:

➡ Does this item measure the specific skills?

➡ Is the reading skill required by this item below students' ability?

➡ Will only a single or very homogeneous set of responses provide a correct response to the item?

➡ Does the item use grammatical structure and vocabulary that is different from that contained in the source of instruction?

➡ If the item requires a numerical response, does the question state the unit of measurement to be used in the answer?

➡ Does the blank represent a key word?

➡ Are blanks placed at or near the end of the item?

➡ Is the number of blanks sufficiently limited?

Constructed response items "are assessment items that ask students to apply knowledge, skills, and critical thinking abilities to real-world, standards-driven performance tasks" (Tankersley, 2007, p. 3). There are a range of options with constructed response and the short answer questions discussed above could be considered a type of constructed response. More commonly, these items include open-ended questions that require students to consider the question and what they know. Often these questions require students to apply what they have learned. For example, fourth-grade teacher Jessie Russell asked his students a few questions of this type about the book *Shiloh* (Naylor, 2000):

➡ How did Shiloh change Marty's character?

➡ Why do you think Judd makes Marty work so hard?

➡ Should Marty have told his father about the deer? Why or why not?

Notice that students would have to draw from different parts of the book or consider information beyond that which is right there in the text to be able to answer these questions. The teacher would need to read each response and consider the knowledge the student has demonstrated. Of course, these items favor students who have a stronger command of English and may mask the knowledge of students who have difficulty composing in English.

We provide this information for one reason: If tests are going to be used, they should be well developed. Tests have been vilified of late, but they are one way of understanding the world. We see tests as a genre. They may not be your favorite genre, but they are one way of organizing information. And students will likely encounter tests for the rest of their lives (such as when they want to drive a car, work in a restaurant, advance in a career, or become licensed). That does not mean that assessment should be limited to tests but rather that they can be used in distance and blended learning with some planning.

Technology-Enhanced Tests

Keelie Bauman uses PlayPosit to create a science lesson and display quiz questions.

resources.corwin.com/ AssessmentPlaybook

There are a number of systems that allow for increased technology use in assessing learning. For example, there are systems that allow for quiz questions to be embedded into videos, such as PlayPosit, EdPuzzle, and Nearpod. Each of these has strengths and can be evaluated for the appropriateness to your classroom. Our point is not to recommend one platform over another, but to recognize that there are options in distance and blended learning to use technology in assessment.

For example, middle school history teacher Tyler Carlyle creates short videos that include images from medieval times and imports them into PlayPosit. When his students watch the videos, they are required to respond to the questions he has created. These questions pop up on the left side of their screen and the video freezes until they respond. The system tracks student responses for later analysis. Mr. Carlyle allows his students to watch the videos several times, if they want, to obtain the scores that they want.

We should also note that there are a number of intelligent tutoring systems that rely on assessment information to provide students with additional practice. These systems rely on student responses to assessment items and many have algorithms to increase the complexity of items as students' progress through their tutoring experiences.

Error Analysis

An interesting twist on tests was presented by mathematics teacher Harold Mandel-baum. He provided his students a test, but the entire test had already been completed. As he said to his students in the video that accompanied the test, "You'll notice that the entire test has been completed for you. Your task is to analyze the test because this person has made some errors. Please find the errors and let me know why you believe that this person made the specific error. Think about the cause of the error. What think-ing might have gone wrong to produce this type of error?"

As Mr. Mandelbaum noted, this task requires that students engage in error analysis, which is fairly complex skill for students and one that requires fairly sophisticated con-ceptual knowledge. He also said that he could easily change the errors and was able to create ten different version of the assessment in a matter of minutes. In his words, "I had never thought about this until I was distance teaching. I wanted to figure out a way to understand students' thinking so that I would know where their misconceptions were. I learned a lot about my students, and I think that this will be a format for the tests I give no matter what the format of schooling is."

Read Alouds

For younger students, it's useful to listen to them read as part of the assessment pro-cess. These read alouds allow you to confirm that students are applying the rules of language and not simply guessing at words or relying on pictures to make decisions about the content. In distance learning, we can recruit parents to collect short videos of their children reading aloud and then we can use those recordings to monitor prog-ress and confirm that the instruction has had an impact. There is evidence going back several decades that suggests that young children should read aloud to pets or stuffed animals as it can improve fluency as well as attitudes toward reading (e.g., Francis, 2009; Newlin, 2003) not to mention a range of social and emotional skills. But for our purpose here, inviting children to read aloud daily is a good practice. And collecting samples of that reading is useful in your assessment efforts. As a kindergarten teacher told us, "Not all of the families of the children in my class can do this, but I get about 60 percent to 75 percent per week. And that means my synchronous time is not spent on assessment other than the few students whose parents were not able to capture the video for me. I watch those videos to figure out how to group students and to see what impact the instruction has had."

Essays

Essays provide students with opportunities to elaborate and provide more detailed answers. It's hard to guess on an essay but it is still possible to cheat as there are many services available to pay for an essay to be completed. Essays can take the form of a term paper, or in some cases a reproduced essay in a timed secured environment. From a distance, this task can be completed with relative ease for both the teacher and the student. We would like to note, however, that having students perform this task should not occur in isolation. It is of the utmost importance that over the course of the year or semester that students gradually work toward this assessment through composition type of assignments (see Playlist 3, Assessment Through Composing). Having students compose small writing activities can allow us to make reasoned judgments as to where we need to take them next, before evaluating their learning. It is very possible that jumping directly into a major writing assignment such as this without preparation can yield inaccurate assessment results. When students are ready for an essay assessment, it's critical that the prompt be clear. Too many students do poorly if they do not understand the prompt—ensuring clarity about what you want students to focus on is important, unless you want to measure students' ability to work out what you really want by obscure questions.

Students interpret writing tasks quite differently from one another, and this variance influences the product (Flower, 1990). Moreover, novice writers rely on prior knowledge of writing schemas and may not closely examine the task they are being asked to do. Therefore, while the assignment may ask the writer to analyze and interpret, the novice writer may simply summarize, focusing instead on a familiar format such as the ubiquitous five-paragraph essay. These schemata are not simply "untaught"; they must be confronted intentionally.

We see this happen routinely in our own English class. One of the first major pieces we taught in the school year was an analysis of the short story "Every Little Hurricane" by Sherman Alexie (1994). Over a three-day period, we used close reading, annotation, and text-based discussion focusing on the themes of disruption and marginalization in a Native American community. On the fourth day, students completed a ninety-minute, 500-word essay in class using this prompt:

> How does our social and cultural community shape who we are? After reading "Every Little Hurricane" by Sherman Alexie, identify one or more themes and provide specific evidence from the text to support your analysis. Remember to apply insight by citing small but important details and address the complicated issues that Alexie raises in the short story.

We were confident—we had taught a solid series of lessons, the students were engaged, and the discussions were sophisticated. They had completed beautifully annotated

WHEN STUDENTS ARE READY FOR AN ESSAY ASSESSMENT, IT'S CRITICAL THAT THE PROMPT BE CLEAR.

texts to utilize in the construction of their essays. We watched our students carefully for signs of distress, offering quiet assistance as needed. The help some of them needed was surprising. Despite instruction and a writing prompt that were aligned, many of our students wanted to write personal responses. Keisha, a solid student and good writer, had begun her essay with a detailed discussion of the difficulties her cousin experienced in middle school. Although the task itself did not invite personal response, she had relied on a familiar writing schema. After all, hadn't she been encouraged for twelve years to write in this fashion? It was only after parsing the prompt and linking it to the lessons and her annotations that she was able to develop a plan that more accurately addressed the task.

A suitably designed writing prompt should guide students in developing their essay. As such, the basic components of a writing assignment or prompt are

1. The topic

2. The audience

3. The rhetorical structure or genre to be produced

Oliver (1995) studied the effects of these prompt elements on the writing of middle and high school students, examining the interaction of audience, task, and rhetorical style to determine what worked best as writers developed. She found that middle school students did best when the prompt specified the audience, real or contrived, and when the topic statement was simpler (e.g., "Make a recommendation to a fellow seventh-grade student."). Ninth-grade writers were better equipped to handle more detailed information about the topic itself (e.g., "Discuss the causes and effects of water desalination on the marine ecology."), while eleventh-grade writers in the study did best when information about the rhetorical structure was elaborated (e.g., "Select a position on the topic of stem cell research and write an argumentative essay that describes your position and offers counterarguments."). It should be noted that all three components—audience, topic, and rhetorical specification—should be present in a well-designed writing prompt. However, Oliver's findings provide more nuanced information about their relative weighting within a writing prompt.

Skilled writers (1) establish their own writing goals; (2) utilize needed textual, rhetorical, or writing processes; and (3) are aware of the need to do both in order to write (Flower, 1990). A good writing assignment or prompt should lend itself to this type of student analysis. Therefore, the student should be able to parse a writing assignment such that they can answer the following questions:

➡ What is my purpose for writing this piece?

➡ Who is my audience?

➡ What is the task?

The Literacy Design Collaborative (www.ldc.org) suggests that good writing prompts can be formulated using prefabricated task templates that allow the teacher to customize.

For example, the following argumentation task template invites students to compare two conditions:

> [Insert question] After reading _____ (literature or informational texts), write a/an _____ (essay or substitute) that compares_____ (content) and argues _____ (content). Be sure to support your position with evidence from the texts.

This template can be used as a springboard for writing in any number of subject areas. In each case, the writing task specifies the purpose and task in detail. We have augmented these prompts with explicitly stated information about audiences in order to further support students as they craft their pieces:

- **ELA:** <u>What is courage in a time of war?</u> After reading <u>Stephen Crane's *Red Badge of Courage*</u>, write an <u>essay for peers</u> that compares <u>Henry Fleming's inner conflict as he wrestles with moral and ethical issues of war</u> and <u>argues for a definition of true courage</u>. Be sure to support your position with evidence from the text.

- **US History:** <u>What is the cost of freedom?</u> After reading <u>*Korematsu v. United States*, 323 U.S. 214 (1944), the Supreme Court decision upholding the internment of Japanese and Japanese-Americans during World War II</u>, write an <u>essay for fellow high school history students</u> that compares <u>the cases brought by the plaintiff and defendant</u> and argues <u>whether the court ruled rightly or wrongly on its constitutionality</u>. Be sure to support your position with evidence from the text.

- **Science:** <u>Is the expense of interplanetary exploration worth the cost?</u> After reading the article, <u>"Mars Rover Curiosity's Siblings: A Short History of Landings On Alien Planets" by Clay Dillow</u>, write a <u>fact guide for potential voters</u> that compares <u>the knowledge gained with the cost in doing so</u> and argues <u>its worth to humankind</u>. Be sure to support your position with evidence from the text.

istock/SyhinStas

For younger students, it's useful to listen to them read as part of the assessment process.

The writing assignment or prompt should not be an afterthought, tacked on in haste to the end of a unit. Rather, reading and discussion tasks should be aligned with the culminating task itself so that students can more strategically engage in inquiry throughout the unit.

Of course, these need to be graded and that takes time. Analytic or holistic rubrics can help students focus on the aspects that need attention. In distance and blended learning, teachers are using audio feedback such as Google Voice to share their feedback with students. We recommend using text-matching software such as Turnitin with each essay. Students should learn to analyze the similarity reports and recognize that attribution of sources is a critical aspect of their responses.

Screenshots

➡ Evaluations of learning require that we confirm students' understanding.

➡ The tools we can use to confirm students learning each have advantages and disadvantages.

➡ Trust in students is important, as is reducing the opportunities students have to outsource their assessments.

UPGRADE 4: THINK LIKE AN EVALUATOR

Thus far, we have focused on a wide range of tools that are useful in assessing students' learning. We have implied that teachers can do things with the assessment information. In this upgrade, we focus more specifically on what those things might be. There are two mindframes from Visible Learning that guide this upgrade (Hattie & Zierer, 2018):

➔ I am an evaluator of my impact on student learning.

➔ I see assessment as informing my impact and next steps.

Together, these mindframes suggest that you should use the assessment data you collect for more than writing report cards or assigning grades. We realize that you are required to do that. But there is more to be done with the data that we collect. As noted in these mindframes, next steps are influenced by the analysis of the data. And the data can be used to determine the impact of the learning experiences that have been planned. Both of these are important aspects of assessment.

Determining Impact

Did students learn something from the lesson? How much did they learn? Could they have learned more? These questions gnaw even as we design learning experiences. For most of us who are teaching in distance and blended formats, our "tried-and-true" lessons need to be adjusted or redesigned. And we're left wondering if they worked. When we see evidence that our lessons work, our sense of efficacy is increased and we're happier with our jobs. When we do not know if our lessons are effective, our sense of efficacy can be reduced and we are at risk of burnout, which occurs when we do not see an impact from our efforts. Jerald (2007) noted that teachers with strong self-efficacy

➔ Tend to exhibit greater levels of planning and organization

➔ Are more open to new ideas and are more willing to experiment with new methods to better meet the needs of their students

➔ Are more persistent and resilient when things do not go smoothly

➔ Are less critical of students when they make errors

➔ Are less inclined to refer a difficult student to special education (Protheroe, 2008, p. 43)

Over time, as teachers discuss the data and success with their peers, they develop collective teacher efficacy. Goddard, Hoy, and Hoy (2000) define collective teacher efficacy as "the perceptions of teachers in a school that the efforts of the faculty as a whole will have a positive effect on students" with staff agreeing that "teachers in this school can get through to the most difficult students" (p. 480). This asks for teachers to think aloud about their interpretations of progress, their conceptions of high expectations, and to use evidence (from tests, from student voice, from artifacts of student work) to illustrate these notions of impact, progress, and expectations. It is the role of other teachers to critique these mindframes, which emphasizes the important role of school leaders to create staff rooms and professional learning opportunities based on high trust, intellectual safety, and a sense of collective impact on the learning for all in the school.

Determining impact is fairly simple. It's more than a self-report or a hunch. It's based on analysis of data. Remember, we're thinking like evaluators, so we review data. We recommend that teachers calculate an effect size to check on the impact of their efforts. The process of calculating an effect size is fairly simple. Before we discuss that, it's important to remember a few things:

1. **Lessons should have clear learning intentions**. It's hard to determine whether students have learned something if they (and we) aren't sure what it was they were supposed to learn.

2. **Lessons should have clear success criteria**. The success criteria provide the tools necessary to assess learning. If the success criteria involve writing about history, then learning has to involve both writing and content area learning. Sometimes teachers conflate success criteria and are unable to determine if students have learned something, even when they have.

3. **The success criteria indicate what quality looks like**. To determine whether or not learning has occurred, students and teachers have to know what success looks like. If students believe that good enough is sufficient, they may only reach for that level. When they understand what excellent work looks like, they can reach higher.

4. **Students should know where they stand in relation to the criteria for success**. When students have no idea if they've done well or not, learning is compromised. Students should understand that learning is on a continuum, that errors are opportunities to learn, and that they can learn more.

With these four conditions in place, teachers are ready to examine the impact of the learning experience. An effect size requires that we have two data sources for each student: before and after the instruction or intervention. Without initial assessment information, there may be evidence that students know and can do stuff, but you cannot attribute that to the learning experiences. Maybe they already knew it before the lessons. Diagnose and discover early. Determining impact requires that we know the starting place for each student.

Initial assessment. It's easy to overlook the initial assessment and accept achievement as learning. But without early assessment, becoming a better teacher and designer of amazing learning situations is left to chance. For example, Amanda Nichols assessed students' number sense, specifically the aspects of oral counting and number identification, during the first week of November. These are important skills. Ms. Nichols noted that all but two of her students could count to 20. That's their current achievement. It doesn't tell her anything about the impact of her teaching or the

> DETERMINING IMPACT REQUIRES THAT WE KNOW THE STARTING PLACE FOR EACH STUDENT.

lessons she designed on their learning because she did not have a baseline. What if the majority of the class had attended a strong transitional kindergarten class and already knew how to count? In that case, the time devoted to counting was a waste. What if none of her students could count to 20 at the onset of the year? In that case, the lessons were probably pretty powerful, and she might want to share them with her grade-level team. This kindergarten example highlights a missing part of many teachers' instructional practices. Failing to identify what students know and can do at the outset of a unit of study blocks any ability to determine if learning has occurred and thus any ability for there to be a discussion about effective instruction and intervention.

Armed with baseline, initial assessment information, teachers can design instructional interventions to close the gap between what students already know and what they are expected to learn. In this case, time is used more precisely because specific strategies can be selected based on the type of learning needed.

Post-Assessment. Once the lessons have been completed, teachers administer an assessment. It can be the same assessment, or it can be based on the same ideas. This opens the door to an investigation about impact. Did the lessons that were taught change students? That is learning.

When the initial and post-test data are available, the effect size can be determined. As an example, Figure 31 contains the scores from a middle school class. Lelia Chavez was focused on teaching homonyms, homophones, and homographs. To calculate an effect size, first determine the average for the initial assessment and the average for the post-assessment. It's easy to do this in an Excel spreadsheet. Here's how:

➡ Type the students' names in one column.

➡ Type their scores for the initial and post-assessments in other columns.

➡ Highlight the column with the pre-assessment scores and select the "average" tool and place the average at the bottom of that column.

➡ Do the same for the post-assessment column.

In Ms. Chavez's example, the average initial assessment score was 11 meaning that, on average, students knew 11 of the items out of 20 prior to instruction. For two months, students were introduced to different words that met the criteria of homonyms, homophones, and homographs. Each day, as part of her asynchronous lessons, students practiced their knowledge of these types of words (among many other things that they learned). In addition, they were encouraged to play with these words in their writing. Wanting to know if this was an area of improvement, Ms. Chavez gave students another assessment. In this case, the examples were totally different and, like the initial assessment were randomly generated from a test bank that was included with the textbook adoption. The post-assessment average was 16. Is that a worthy impact? It's hard to judge because a few points average growth doesn't sound very impressive; so, you need to calculate the effect size.

The next step in determining the effect size is to calculate standard deviation. Excel will do this as well:

1. Type =STDEV.P and then select the student scores in the pre-assessment column again.
2. Do the same in the post-assessment column.
3. Subtract the pre-assessment from the post-assessment and then divide by the standard deviation.*

Here's the formula:

$$\text{Effect size} = \frac{\text{Average (post-assessment)}-\text{Average (pre-assessment)}}{\text{Average standard deviation or SD*}}$$

*You can quickly calculate standard deviation on a number of websites, such as graphpad .com/quickcalcs/CImean1.cfm.

31 EFFECT SIZE CALCULATION

Name	Pre	Post	Individual Effect Size	
Alexander	12	18	2.61	
Alexis	12	12	0.00	
Alyssa	8	16	3.48	
Ana	8	17	4.35	
Andrea	7	11	1.74	
Angel	12	16	1.74	
Bianca	12	18	2.61	
Caitlin	9	11	0.87	
Elena	15	16	0.44	
Elisabeth	9	17	3.48	
Emir	8	16	3.48	
Gabriel	14	16	0.87	
Giovanni	12	20	3.48	
Irvin	9	15	2.61	
Isaiah	11	16	2.18	
Jerod	11	16	2.18	
Jorge	14	18	1.74	
Jose	12	17	2.18	

(Continued)

(Continued)

Name	Pre	Post	Individual Effect Size	
Joshua	10	17	3.05	
Kassandra	12	18	2.61	
Keneni	9	16	3.05	
Komad	14	20	2.61	
Makala	12	16	1.74	
Marla	16	13	−1.31	
Michael	14	17	1.31	
Nick	12	17	2.18	
Santiago	11	16	2.18	
Shakira	14	16	0.87	
Veronica	16	17	0.44	
Wendy	9	17	3.48	
Yasmin	14	20	2.61	
Average	11.59	16.32		
Standard Deviation	2.43	2.16		2.30
Effect size	1.36			

In the example found in Figure 31, the standard deviation for the pre-assessment is 2.43 and the standard deviation for the post-assessment is 2.16. The average of the two is 2.30. When the effect size is calculated using the formula above, it comes to 1.36, which is a strong impact. Just as critical for Ms. Chavez is to then investigate those students who were below and above this average in her class—and ask why she had positive effects on some students and less on others. Effect sizes provide the critical first step—the evidence, then the hard part happens—the interpretation. If surprised by the different effect sizes, then Ms. Chavez needs to triangulate by using other forms of assessment or revisit some students to seek more evidence of learning.

Thus, Ms. Chavez can conclude her efforts to improve students' language skills were successful. She can then infer that the asynchronous lessons worked. As a note of caution, effect sizes do not establish causation. Ms. Chavez cannot say with confidence that these specific actions caused the student's new understanding, but she should be encouraged to share her approach with others so that they can determine the impact it might have on their students.

Importantly, when the sample sizes are small, or the content being measured is very narrow (e.g., vocabulary compared to deep understanding), or the timeframe is relatively short, it's hard to say how large the effect size should be. In the published research, with larger sample sizes and numerous controls, the average effect size is 0.40. We are not sure what the effect size could or should be for the type of lessons that Ms. Chavez taught, which is why we emphasize looking more at the students above and below the average of your class as a more worthwhile starting point. Such analysis helps understand those students who are increasingly proficient in their use of homonyms, homophones, and homographs and that she should be proud of her efforts. More teaching work is needed for those below the average of the class. It's also important to look at outlier students. For example, Alexis made no growth and Maria performed lower on the post-assessment. Ms. Chavez would be wise to investigate those situations as well as those who still performed below the average.

And this is the impact of thinking like an evaluator. The data allow you to take note and to take action. Ms. Chavez can provide additional instruction to some of her students to accelerate their learning. We intentionally selected a very small part of the overall content Ms. Chavez taught to make a point. We can determine our impact on any aspect of instruction that we want. Ms. Chavez wanted to know if the efforts that she was putting into developing videos for asynchronous learning were a good use of her time, so she selected one area that she was working on as a test case.

As she noted, "I wanted to see if my efforts were worth anything. I recorded videos each day and I can tell my students were watching them. I think we focused on like over 200 homonyms, homophones, and homographs. It was fun for me to play with these words and provide students with quick assessments. I also enjoyed seeing these words appearing in their writing. But, really, it was just good to see that my efforts were working. I want to evaluate other parts of my blended learning as well, but this was a real confidence booster."

> THE DATA ALLOW YOU TO TAKE NOTE AND TO TAKE ACTION.

Taking Action:
Next Steps Instruction

Evaluators look for patterns. When you have assessment information, identify the patterns so that you can figure out what still needs to be done to ensure students are learning. As we noted in Section 1, Assessment Cookies, it's important to know what you want to do with the assessment information before you develop and implement the assessment. In large part, assessment data should be used to drive additional learning. This occurs when we use assessment information formatively. There are other times that we use assessment information to determine what has been learned such that we can fulfill our responsibilities in writing report cards and assigning grades.

In either case, we are evaluators. We use data to determine our impact and to make evaluative decisions. In *The Distance Learning Playbook* (Fisher, Frey, & Hattie, 2020), we introduced an instructional framework for designing learning experiences in remote and blended learning. We noted that some of the moves teachers made occurred asynchronously and other moves occurred during synchronous learning. Both are important. And both are based on the collection and analysis of assessment information. Figure 32 is a visual representation of the instruction framework we discovered. Note that we have added assessment as the wind that drives the pinwheel. Assessment

32 A DISTANCE LEARNING INSTRUCTIONAL FRAMEWORK

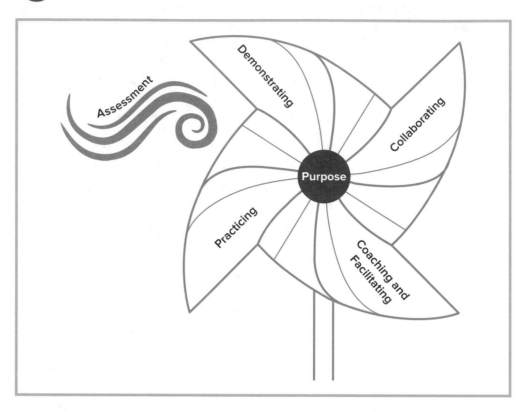

Source: Adapted from Fisher, D., Frey, N., & Hattie, J. (2020). *The distance learning playbook, grades K–12: Teaching for engagement and impact in any setting.* Thousand Oaks, CA: Corwin. Wind image courtesy of Pixabay.

information allows teachers to make instructional decisions such that their impact is increased. A few examples are in order.

Let's say that the teacher collected and analyzed some writing from students and that these analyses revealed that the vast majority of the class failed to include evidence for their claims. As a result, the teacher may decide to record some additional asynchronous demonstration lessons that students could view as needed. As part of the video lesson, the teacher let students know that she was doing this based on her review of student papers. In addition, this teacher may plan some additional coaching sessions for her students so that she can prompt their thinking. In each coaching session, she reviewed the reason for the lesson, noting that there was a gap in the learning that they were going to work on. Over time, the teacher will probably ask students to complete additional practice.

As another example, consider the teacher who in the chat saw that students were confused. When he asked them for a hand signal, they indicated little understanding. In this case, he let them know that he would review the learning intention and success criteria and then reexplain (demonstrate) the lesson before asking students again if they had a better sense of what they were learning. After doing so, he asked students if his decision was useful in helping them understand.

As still another example, consider the teacher who noted that students did not do well on their PlayPosit video quiz. In this case, he decided to assign some additional readings and planned to have students read the texts collaboratively in breakout rooms as they took notes about what their peers thought about the text. As he noted, "I heard some confusion in the video responses, and I thought it would be a good idea to do some review based on the questions that seemed to give us the most trouble."

In each case, the assessment data provided the teacher with information that was used to take action. And in each case, students are likely to learn more when teachers align their instruction with the needs of the students, as evidenced in the data they have collected. In other words, it's an ongoing cycle of collecting data, reviewing and analyzing the data, and then making decisions. In doing so, we get students closer and closer to understanding.

STUDENTS ARE LIKELY TO LEARN MORE WHEN TEACHERS ALIGN THEIR INSTRUCTION WITH THE NEEDS OF THE STUDENTS.

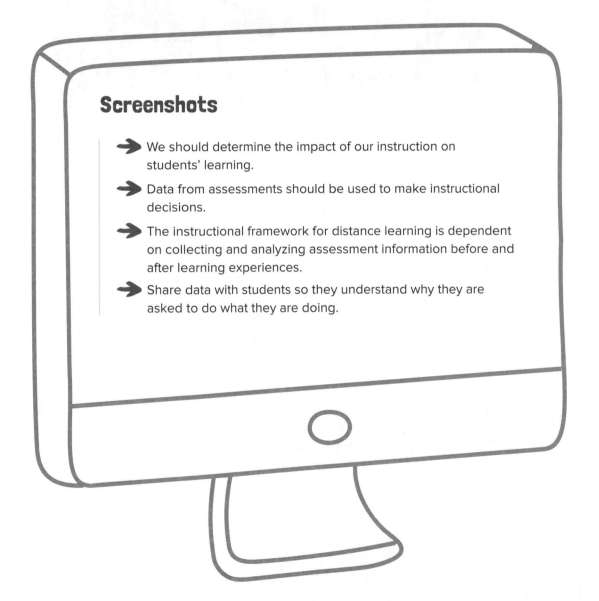

Screenshots

➡ We should determine the impact of our instruction on students' learning.

➡ Data from assessments should be used to make instructional decisions.

➡ The instructional framework for distance learning is dependent on collecting and analyzing assessment information before and after learning experiences.

➡ Share data with students so they understand why they are asked to do what they are doing.

istock/AJ_Watt

The data allow you to take note and take action.

Final Thoughts

The chief purpose of assessment of student learning is to answer the following question: *How do we know our students have learned this?* Due to the circumstance of teaching during a pandemic, we have been challenged to reframe thinking around assessment and instruction. As John has noted, we are in the midst of the greatest unplanned experiment in education. Let's not let what we are learning go to waste. Consider the disconnect between a traditional approach to education and the rapidly changing world we live in. It does seem that, in certain cases, our classrooms have not been as reflective as they might be of the world our students will be living in, and in certain cases, our assessments do not reflect that world either. Much as education evolves, our thinking around assessment must necessarily evolve, too. We are all learning to flex our assessment muscles in new and creative ways. Let's develop a new syntax for schooling that leverages what we are learning to help young people achieve their aspirations.

References

Adesope, O. O., Trevisan, D. A., & Sundararajan, N. (2017). Rethinking the use of tests: A meta-analysis of practice testing. *Review of Educational Research, 87*(3), 659–701.

Alexie, S. (1994). Every little hurricane. In S. Alexie, *The Lone Ranger and Tonto fistfight in heaven* (pp. 1–11). New York, NY: Harper Perennial.

Almarode, J., Fisher, D., Frey, N., & Thunder, K. (2021). *Success criteria playbook.* Thousand Oaks, CA: Corwin.

Andrade, H. G., & Boulay, B. A. (2003). Role of rubric-referenced self-assessment in learning to write. *Journal of Educational Research, 97*, 21–34.

Biggs, J. (1999). *Teaching for quality learning at university.* Buckingham, England: Society for Research into Higher Education and Open University Press.

Boelts, M. (2016). *A bike like Sergio's.* Somerville, MA: Candlewick Press.

Chi, M. T. H. (2000). Self-explaining expository texts: The dual processes of generating inferences and repairing mental models. In R. Glaser (Ed.), *Advances in instructional psychology: Educational design and cognitive science* (pp. 161–238). Mahwah, NJ: Erlbaum.

Chi, M. T. H., Glaser, R., & Farr, M. J. (Eds.) (1988). *The nature of expertise.* Mahwah, NJ: Erlbaum.

Clay, M. M. (2013). *An observation survey of early literacy achievement* (3rd ed.). Portsmouth, NH: Heinemann.

Danielson, C., & Abrutyn, L. (1997). *An introduction to using portfolios in the classroom.* Alexandria, VA: ASCD.

Ebbinghaus, H. (1913). *Memory: A contribution to experimental psychology* (H. A. Ruger & C. E. Bussenius, Trans.). New York, NY: Teachers College, Columbia University. (Original work published 1885)

Fearn, L., & Farnan, N. (2001). *Interactions: Teaching writing and the language arts.* Boston, MA: Houghton Mifflin.

Ferlazzo, L. (2010, June 16). My revised final exams (and an important lesson). *Larry Ferlazzo's Websites of the Day.* Retrieved from http://larryferlazzo.edublogs.org/2010/06/16/my-revised-final-exams/

Fisher, D., Frey, N., & Akhavan, N. (2018). *This is balanced literacy, grades K–6.* Thousand Oaks, CA: Corwin.

Fisher, D., Frey, N., Amador, O., & Assof, J. (2018). *The teacher clarity playbook, grades K–12: A hands-on guide to creating learning intentions and success criteria for organized, effective instruction.* Thousand Oaks, CA: Corwin.

Fisher, D., Frey, N., & Gonzalez Ojeda, A. (2020). *On-your-feet guide: Distance learning by design, grades 3–12.* Thousand Oaks, CA: Corwin.

Fisher, D., Frey, N., & Hattie, J. (2016). *Visible Learning for literacy: Implementing the practices that work best to accelerate student learning.* Thousand Oaks, CA: Corwin.

Fisher, D., Frey, N., & Hattie, J. (2017). *Teaching literacy in the visible learning classroom, grades K–5.* Thousand Oaks, CA: Corwin.

Fisher, D., Frey, N., & Hattie, J. (2020). *The distance learning playbook, grades K–12: Teaching for engagement and impact in any setting.* Thousand Oaks, CA: Corwin.

Fisher, D., Frey, N., & Law, N. (2020). *Comprehension: The skill, will, and thrill of reading.* Thousand Oaks, CA: Corwin.

Flavell, J. H. (1985). *Cognitive development.* Upper Saddle River, NJ: Prentice Hall.

Flower, L. (1990). Studying cognition in context. In L. Flower, V. Stein, J. Ackerman, M. J. Kantz, K. McCormick, & W. C. Peck (Eds.), *Reading-to-Write: Exploring a cognitive and social process* (pp. 3–32). New York, NY: Oxford University Press.

Francis, A., (2009). Thursdays with MacGyver. *Children & Libraries: The Journal of the Association for Library Service to Children, 7*(2), 50–52.

Frey, N., Hattie, J., & Fisher, D. (2018). *Developing assessment-capable visible learners, grades K–12: Maximizing skill, will, and thrill.* Thousand Oaks, CA: Corwin.

Gambrell, L. B. (1983). The occurrence of think-time during reading comprehension instruction. *The Journal of Educational Research, 77*(2), 77–80.

Ghaffar, M. A., Khairallah, M., & Salloum, S. (2020). Co-constructed rubrics and assessment for learning: The impact on middle school students' attitudes and writing skills. *Assessing Writing*, *45*. Advance online publication. Retrieved from https://doi.org/10.1016/j.asw.2020.100468

Goddard, R. D., Hoy, W. K., & Hoy, A. W. (2000). Collective teacher efficacy: Its meaning, measure, and impact on student achievement. *American Educational Research Journal, 37*, 479–507.

Gollwitzer, P. M. (1999). Implementation intentions: Strong effects of simple plans. *American Psychologist, 54*, 493–503.

Hattie, J. (2009). *Visible Learning: A synthesis of over 800 meta-analyses relating to achievement.* New York, NY: Routledge.

Hattie, J., Fisher, D., Frey, N., Gojak, L. M., Moore, S. D., & Mellman, W. (2016). *Visible learning for mathematics, grades K–12: What works best to optimize student learning.* Thousand Oaks, CA: Corwin.

Hattie, J. (n.d.). *Global research database.* Visible Learning Meta[X]. Retrieved from https://www.visiblelearningmetax.com/Influences

Hattie, J., & Zierer, K. (2018). *10 mindframes for Visible Learning: Teaching for success.* New York, NY: Routledge.

Haydon, T., Marsicano, R., & Scott, T. (2013). A comparison of choral and individual responding: A review of the literature. *Preventing School Failure, 57*(4), 181–188.

Hellebrandt, J., & Russell, J. D. (1993). Confirmative evaluation of instructional materials and learners. *Performance + Instruction, 32*(6), 22–27.

Hsia, L., Huang, I., & Hwang, G. (2016). A web-based peer-assessment approach to improving junior high school students' performance, self-efficacy and motivation in performing arts courses. *British Journal of Educational Technology, 47*(4), 618–632.

Isaacs, T., Zara, C., Herbert, G., Coombs, S. J., & Smith, C. (2013). Ipsative assessment. In T. Isaacs, C. Zara, G. Herbert, S. J. Coombs, & C. Smith, *The SAGE key Concepts Series: Key concepts in educational assessment* (pp. 80–82). Thousand Oaks, CA: SAGE.

Israel, E. (2002). Examining multiple perspectives in literature. In J. Holden & J. S. Schmit, (Eds.), *Inquiry and the literary text: Constructing discussions in the English classroom* (pp. 89–103). Urbana, IL: National Council of Teachers of English.

Jerald, C. D. (2007). *Believing and achieving* [Issue brief]. Washington, DC: Center for Comprehensive School Reform and Improvement. Retrieved from https://files.eric.ed.gov/fulltext/ED495708.pdf

Koskinen, P. S., Gambrell, L. B., Kapinus, B. A., & Heathington, B. S. (1988). Retelling: A strategy for enhancing students' reading comprehension. *Reading Teacher, 41*, 892–896.

MacArthur, C. A. (2013). Best practices in teaching evaluation and revision. In S. Graham, C. A. MacArthur, & J. Fitzgerald (Eds.), *Best practices in writing instruction* (2nd ed.; pp. 215–237). New York, NY: Guilford Press.

MacArthur, C. A., Graham, S., & Harris, K. R. (2004). Insights from instructional research on revision with struggling writers. In L. Allal, L. Chanquoy, & P. Largy (Eds.), *Revision: Cognitive and instructional processes* (pp. 125–137). Norwell, MA: Kluwer.

McAllister, D., & Guidice, R. M. (2012). This is only a test: A machine-graded improvement to the multiple-choice and true-false examination. *Teaching in Higher Education, 17*(2), 193–207.

Morrow, L. M. (1985). Retelling stories: A strategy for improving children's comprehension, concept of story structure, and oral language complexity. *Elementary School Journal, 85*, 647–661.

Naylor, P. R. (2000). *Shiloh*. New York, NY: Aladdin.

Newlin, R. B. (2003). Paws for reading. *School Library Journal, 49*(6), 43.

Nordengren, C. (2019). Goal-setting practices that support a learning culture. *Phi Delta Kappan, 101*(1), 18–22.

Nuthall, G. (2006). *Hidden lives of learners*. Wellington: New Zealand Council for Educational Research Press.

Oliver, E. (1995). The writing quality of seventh, ninth, and eleventh graders, and college freshmen: Does rhetorical specification in writing prompts make a difference? *Research In The Teaching Of English, 29*(4), 422–450.

Oosterhof, A., Conrad, R. M., & Ely, D. P. (2008). *Assessing learners online*. Upper Saddle River, NJ: Merrill/Prentice Hall.

Patall, E. A., Cooper, H., & Robinson, J. C. (2008). The effects of choice on intrinsic motivation and related outcomes: A meta-analysis of research findings. *Psychological Bulletin, 134*, 270–300.

Potash, B. (2019, May 26). *A simple trick for success with one-pagers*. Retrieved from https://www.cultofpedagogy.com/one-pagers/

Protheroe, N. (2008, May). Teacher efficacy: What is it and does it matter? *Principal*, 42–45.

Randolph, J. J. (2007). Meta-analysis of the research on response cards: Effects on test achievement, quiz achievement, participation, and off-task behavior. *Journal of Positive Behavior Interventions, 9*(2), 113–128.

Reinholz, D. L. (2018). Peer feedback for learning mathematics. *American Mathematical Monthly, 125*(7), 653–658.

Reynolds, J. (2019). *Look both ways: A tale told in ten blocks*. New York, NY: Simon & Schuster.

Roberts, T., & Billings, L. (1999). *The Paideia classroom: Teaching for understanding* (Eye on Education series). New York, NY: Routledge.

Robinson, C. (2018). Guest speakers and mentors for career exploration in the science classroom. *Science Scope, 41*(8), 18–21.

Roediger, H. L., & Karpicke, J. D. (2006). The power of testing memory: Basic research and implications for educational practice. *Perspectives on Psychological Science, 1*, 181–210.

Rollins, S. P. (2014). *Learning in the fast lane*. Alexandria, VA: ASCD.

Sanchez, C. E., Atkinson, K. M., Koenka, A. C., Moshontz, H., & Cooper, H. (2017). Self-grading and peer-grading for formative and summative assessments in 3rd through 12th grade classrooms: A meta-analysis. *Journal of Educational Psychology, 109*(8), 1049–1066.

Schoenfeld, A. H. (1992). Learning to think mathematically: Problem-solving, metacognition, and sense-making in mathematics. In D. Grouws (Ed.), *Handbook for research in mathematics teaching and learning* (pp. 334–370). New York, NY: Macmillan.

Simmons, J. (2003). Responders are taught, not born. *Journal of Adolescent and Adult Literacy, 46*(8), 684–693.

Spinath, B., Spinath, F. M., Harlaar, N., & Plomin, R. (2006). Predicting school achievement from general cognitive ability, self-perceived ability, and intrinsic value. *Intelligence, 34*(4), 363–374.

Stegmann, K., Wecker, C., Weinberger, A., & Fischer, F. (2012). Collaborative argumentation and cognitive elaboration in a computer-supported collaborative learning environment. *Instructional Science, 40*(2), 297–323.

Tankersley, K. (2007). *Tests that teach: Using standardized tests to improve instruction.* Alexandria, VA: ASCD.

Vygotsky, L. S. (1978). *Mind in society: The development of higher psychological processes.* Cambridge, MA: Harvard University Press.

Willingham, D. T. (2003). How to help students see when their knowledge is superficial or incomplete. *American Educator.* Retrieved from https://www.aft.org/ae/winter2003–2004/willingham

Wiseman, R., Fisher, D., Frey, N., & Hattie, J. (2020). *The distance learning playbook for parents: How to support your child's academic, social, and emotional development in any setting.* Thousand Oaks, CA: Corwin.

Xu, X., Kauer, S., & Tupy, S. (2016). Multiple-choice questions: Tips for optimizing assessment in-seat and online. *Scholarship of Teaching and Learning in Psychology, 2*(2), 147–158.

Zimmerman, J., & Robertson, E. (2017). *The case for contention: Teaching controversial issues in American schools.* Chicago, IL: University of Chicago Press.

Index

About the Authors

Douglas Fisher, PhD, is a professor of educational leadership at San Diego State University and a leader at Health Sciences High & Middle College. He has served as a teacher, language development specialist, and administrator in public schools and nonprofit organizations. Doug has engaged in professional learning communities for several decades, building teams that design and implement systems to impact teaching and learning. He has published numerous books on teaching and learning, such as *The Distance Learning Playbook* and the PLC+ series.

Nancy Frey, PhD, is a professor in educational leadership at San Diego State University and a leader at Health Sciences High & Middle College. She has been a special education teacher, reading specialist, and administrator in public schools. Nancy has engaged in professional learning communities as a member and in designing schoolwide systems to improve teaching and learning for all students. She has published numerous books, including *The Distance Learning Playbook* and *The Distance Learning Playbook for College and University Instruction.*

Vince Bustamante, MEd, is an instructional coach, curriculum content developer, and author who currently works for Edmonton Catholic Schools as a social studies curriculum consultant. Holding an MEd from the University of Victoria (Canada) in Curriculum and Instruction, he serves to incorporate research into classroom practice. As a certified Visible Learning+™ consultant, Vince is passionate about assessment, teacher clarity, and creating classroom environments that foster deep learning experiences where teachers understand and evaluate their impact on student learning. He has also co-authored *Great Teaching by Design: From Intention to Implementation in the Visible Learning Classroom.*

John Hattie, PhD, is an award-winning education researcher and best-selling author with nearly 30 years of experience examining what works best in student learning and achievement. His research, better known as Visible Learning®, is a culmination of nearly 30 years synthesizing more than 1,500 meta-analyses comprising more than 90,000 studies involving over 300 million students around the world. His notable publications include *Visible Learning, Visible Learning for Teachers, Visible Learning and the Science of How We Learn,* and *10 Mindframes for Visible Learning.*

A SAGE Publishing Company

Helping educators make the greatest impact

CORWIN HAS ONE MISSION: to enhance education through intentional professional learning.

We build long-term relationships with our authors, educators, clients, and associations who partner with us to develop and continuously improve the best evidence-based practices that establish and support lifelong learning.

Supporting TEACHERS | Empowering STUDENTS

THE TEACHER CLARITY PLAYBOOK

Designed for PLCs or independent teacher use, this playbook guides practitioners to align lessons, objectives, and outcomes of learning seamlessly, so that the classroom hours flow productively for everyone.

THE TEACHER CREDIBILITY AND COLLECTIVE EFFICACY PLAYBOOK

Jumpstart learning and achievement in your classroom by increasing your credibility with students and the collective efficacy of the team of educators at your school.

DEVELOPING ASSESSMENT-CAPABLE VISIBLE LEARNERS

Imagine students who understand their educational goals and monitor their progress. This illuminating book focuses on self-assessment as a springboard for markedly higher levels of student achievement.

PLC+

What makes a powerful and results-driven professional learning community (PLC)? The answer is *PLC+*, a framework that leads educators to question practices, not just outcomes.

THE PLC+ PLAYBOOK

Help your PLC+ group to work wiser, not harder, with this practical guide to planning and implementing PLC+ groups in a collaborative setting.

THE PLC+ ACTIVATOR'S GUIDE

The PLC+ Activator's Guide offers a practical approach and real-life examples that show activators what to expect and how to navigate a successful PLC journey.

Learn more at Corwin.com

Unleash the promise of social learning

No longer is professional learning confined to a specific time or place. With Corwin virtual professional learning, **PD can be everywhere and anywhere you need it.**

Corwin's virtual professional learning options give schools and districts the power to rapidly re-establish professional learning as a critical support to teachers during challenging times and offer flexible ways to engage with peers around urgent problems of practice.

CORWIN Visible Learning+™

Focus on Student Learning

Knowing our impact on students is the cornerstone of Professor John Hattie's research findings. The best laid instructional plans put student learning and teacher impact at the forefront. Focus on student feedback and developing student independence and resilience so that students can monitor their own progress and take ownership of their learning.

CORWIN Teacher Clarity

Get Clear on Instruction

Support teachers in how to provide instruction that is engaging and targeted to student needs. Teachers need clarity on how to best assess where students are in the fall, determine the focus of instructional units, and provide students what they need in meaningful and authentic ways. This is the foundation of effective teaching.

CORWIN PLC+

Rally Your Teachers

Your teachers are your greatest asset. Provide them the structures and processes to collaborate effectively to develop solutions to our most urgent problems of practice. This is a critical first step to ensure teachers work together effectively to support students in the most meaningful way.

Learn more about our virtual PD options at corwin.com/virtualpd